Health, Medicine
AND
Religion

SWAMI BRAHMESHANANDA

Sri Ramakrishna Math
MYLAPORE, CHENNAI 600 004

Published by
The President
Sri Ramakrishna Math
Mylapore, Chennai-4

II-2M 3C-12-2004
ISBN 81-7823-140-9

Printed in India at
Sri Ramakrishna Math Printing Press
Mylapore, Chennai-4

Preface

*D*uring the last few decades, the world of medicine has undergone a sea-change. No more has medicine remained a science and an art as it used to be some fifty years ago. With minimal technical assistance at hand, doctors, both physicians and surgeons, used to achieve miraculous results in diagnosis and treatment, merely with the help of their clinical acumen, insight, determination and pure human skill. That is why we have called medicine a science and an art. But now technicalization, commercialization and globalization have radically changed the scene.

Medical technology is probably the most advanced branch of technology today. Most of the work of diagnosis and treatment, especially surgical, is done today by machines. With the help of technology such miracles as transplantation of heart and kidney, microsurgery of eye and ear, laser treatment of eye diseases etc., have become possible. But it has robbed doctors of human skill and

Publisher's Note

$\mathcal{W}$e are happy to present before the readers, this compilation of articles on the theme of health and medical science in the light of ethics, religion and spirituality, by Swami Brahmeshananda. The author is a trained physician who has personally faced the problem of declining ethical codes in the practice of medicine during his more than three decades of practice as a medical consultant. Though the compiled articles are independent in themselves, and were written during a span of more than fifteen years, they have a common theme: search for values in the field of health and medicine.

The book is primarily addressed to the medical professionals, but we are sure, it will prove enlightening for lay readers too.

—Sri Ramakrishna Math
22 February 2004   Chennai 4
Sri Ramakrishna Jayanti

clinical acumen. Now all the ingenuity finds expression in invention of newer and more sophisticated gadgets. Technicalization has stunted the growth of head and heart of doctors and made them medical technicians.

Technological advancements have strengthened the view of the medical materialists that man is a machine made of complex molecules which works bio-chemically and eletro-magnetically. A patient is looked upon as a disordered machine and his or her psycho-socio-economical dimensions are overlooked. This attitude has badly undermined the ethical and humanitarian aspects of the practice of medicine. There has been further deterioration due to an unprecedented commercialization of medicine in recent years. The magnitude of profit earning through the manufacture, sale and use of medical gadgets and medicines, and through diagnostic investigations, is staggering. No one ever imagined fifty years ago that such a noble and humanitarian branch of human endeavour as medicine would get degraded to such a base lucrative trade. In retrospect, one is amazed at the aptness of Sri Ramakrishna's derogatory remarks about doctors, made more than a century ago. No one feels greater agony and humiliation at this degradation of the medical profession than a conscientious, humanitarian doctor who loves his profession and takes pride in it.

One of the by-products of the commercialization of medicine is the inclusion of medical practice within the purview of the *Consumer Protection Act* in India. On the one hand it has made doctors more alert and careful, but on the other hand, it has seriously undermined the already endangered doctor-patient relationship. The patient is now a consumer who expects full returns for the amount he is paying. While this degradation of relationship is unfortunate and lamentable, the doctors are themselves to blame for it.

Spread of information through the expanding network of audio-visual and print-media, and greater facilities for travels and communication, have, like all others aspects of life, made medicine global. This has led, not only to the spread of medical knowledge, but also of diseases and evils like drug-addiction and AIDS. Malnutrition and return of malaria and multidrug resistant tuberculosis are some of the present day global medical problems. Social and preventive medicine has therefore gained great importance. Medicine has now become a global issue with far-reaching political, social and economical implications.

Of late, medical philosophers have come to the conclusion that modern medicine has reached its acme and that every further advancement will simply lead to a manifold escalation of cost, with comparatively negligible benefits. They have, therefore, turned towards alternative treatment modalities and the result is the evolution of the concept of holistic medicine. Yoga, Ayurveda, Acupuncture, Acupressure, Naturotherapy, Pranic-healing, etc. are becoming popular easpecially in the affluent societies.

Thus, medical profession is at a cross roads today. It is difficult to predict what direction it will take in the future. The onus is on the doctors.

The articles compiled in this book deal with sociological, ethical and spiritual aspects and the lay readers too would appreciate and enjoy them.

—*Swami Brahmeshananda*

Contents

Sri Ramakrishna
and Physicians

$\mathcal{D}$uring his life span of fifty years, Sri Ramakrishna met thousands of men and women belonging to all walks of life. This was necessary for the propagation of his message of universal peace and harmony, which was not meant only for a selected group of disciples belonging to a city or a community. While the main task of spreading broadcast the message of Sri Ramakrishna was done by Swami Vivekananda, who travelled extensively all over India and abroad, Sri Ramakrishna too, while leading a life mostly confined to the city of Kolkata, took great pains himself to meet people of all socio-economic and intellectual status so that he might do the greatest good to the greatest number. And those who in some way or the other came in direct contact with him during his life-time, were indeed blessed. Among these

1

fortunate ones were a number of physicians also.

But while the members of other professions—students, teachers, lawyers, thinkers and preachers—went to Sri Ramakrishna looking upon him as a saint or a prophet, the men of the medical profession paid him visits as their patient also; and with reference to Sri Ramakrishna, the prophet of the age, this doctor-patient relationship has a special significance.

Sri Ramakrishna's Health and Disease

Although the available pictures of Sri Ramakrishna depict him as a frail little man, the fact is that he was an unusually healthy person. Spiritual practices entail tremendous strain upon the nervous, the cardiovascular and the respiratory systems, and unless these are extraordinarily strong, the body breaks down under the strain of Sadhana. Sri Ramakrishna himself used to say that when spiritual emotions manifest in a body, they shatter it just as an elephant shatters a hut made of bamboo and straw. "When Kundalini rises to the Sahasrara and the mind goes into Samadhi, the aspirant loses all consciousness of the outer world. He can no longer retain his physical body. In that state the life breath lingers for twenty one days and then passes out."[1]

Disease, decay and death are, however, inevitable in a physical body in which the processes of anabolism and catabolism are constantly going on. Sri Ramakrishna's body was no exception to this natural law. Once he fell down and broke his arm. At the end of his long period of Sadhana he suffered from severe blood-dysentery for six months which permanently damaged his digestion. And during the last days of his life he suffered from cancer of the larynx.

Apart from these physical ailments, Sri Ramakrishna underwent many bodily changes and physiological manifestations due to high spiritual states. These were mistaken as signs and symptoms of internal physical illnesses and doctors were consulted. In his childhood, he was active, energetic and enjoyed a robust health.

---

1. *The Gospel of Sri Ramakrishna*, Sri Ramakrishna Math, Madras - 4, 1981, p.500.

He became "unconscious" thrice during boyhood because of high spiritual states. This was naturally thought to be due to serious organic illness and his parents must have consulted whatever healers were available in that interior village of Kamarpukur. During the period of Sadhana, Mathurnath Biswas, his caretaker, spared no pains to have him examined by renowned physicians for his bodily symptoms. It was however during the terminal illness that he came in contact with a maximum number of physicians.

The Physicians Who Met Sri Ramakrishna

The physicians who met Sri Ramakrishna belonged to all the disciplines of the medical science. There were homoeopaths, Ayurvedic Kavirajs, men trained in modern western medicine, and even exorcists. Not all exorcists are cheats; some of them are very effective psychotherapists. By their weird antics, they draw the attention of the patient, making him receptive to their suggestions. A good exorcist can bring to the surface repressed conflicts and thus bring about a cure. The divine inebriation of Sri Ramakrishna was so unusual that it was thought he was possessed by an 'evil spirit'. He was therefore shown to a few exorcists who invoked a 'Chanda', who 'certified' that Sri Ramakrishna was not suffering from any mental disease.

On the basis of the nature and duration of their relationship with Sri Ramakrishna, the physicians can be divided into three classes. The first class of physicians met Sri Ramakrishna only in their capacity of doctor, the contact being restricted to the professional visit only. But, however short the contact might have been, Sri Ramakrishna never missed the least opportunity to instill spirituality into them by general talk on spiritual matters or by specific instructions.

The second class consists of those physicians who approached Sri Ramakrishna as spiritual aspirants and sooner or later gave up the medical profession to become his ardent disciples. This group includes those physicians also who may have visited him earlier in the capacity of a doctor, but being impressed by his spirituality, later visited him only for spiritual purposes.

Swami Saradananda, the great monastic disciple of Sri Ramakrishna, had entered the medical school but renounced the world and became a monk without completing the medical studies. Durgacharan Nag, the great householder disciple, was a qualified homoeopath. One day he heard Sri Ramakrishna denounce physicians. He immediately threw away his medical books and box of medicines into the Ganga and gave up the profession for ever. Another disciple of Sri Ramakrishna, Dr. Ramachandra Dutta, was a graduate of the Campbell Medical School, Calcutta, but hardly ever practiced medicine. He became, instead, a renowned and successful chemist-pharmacologist. During the early part of his professional career he was an atheist, but the sudden death of his beloved daughter awoke him to the grim reality of death. He finally found solace at the feet of Sri Ramakrishna.

The case of Dr. Mahendralal Sarkar is different from the two cases of physicians described above, and forms a class in itself. Dr. Sarkar visited Sri Ramakrishna in the capacity of a physician, but his contact was neither short nor restricted to a doctor-patient relationship only. He treated Sri Ramakrishna for months during his last illness and visited him almost every day. While maintaining the privileged position of the treating physician, he cleverly used this opportunity to derive spiritual benefit from the holy company of Sri Ramakrishna. On the pretext of professional visits he spent hours in his blissful company, engaged him in philosophical discussions and enjoyed the singing of devotional songs. Both the patient and the doctor enjoyed each other's company. Although he differed from Sri Ramakrishna on certain philosophical issues, especially on the theory of God incarnating as man, and never professed himself a disciple of Sri Ramakrishna, it was obvious that he was deeply influenced by him spiritually. He also had the unique opportunity of examining Sri Ramakrishna during Samadhi—probably the first ever medical examination of a high Yogic state by a qualified physician.

Sri Ramakrishna as a Patient

Sri Ramakrishna was a good patient and considered the treating physician a

'Narayana' whose instruction must be followed to the letter. Once, for example, when he was asked to abstain from water as a part of diet restriction, he wanted the Holy Mother Sri Sarada Devi to give him even pomegranate seeds free from the least trace of water! At the same time, he had his likes and dislikes regarding physicians. He did not like a physician in particular who pressed his tongue rather too hard while conducting the examination of his throat. When, however, it was told that the doctor did not mean to hurt him, he conceded that the doctor might have done so to make a thorough examination of the throat. He appreciated the quality of humility and a quiet nature in doctors and liked a physician who had these.[1]

At times, Sri Ramakrishna would be impatient like a child regarding his illness. He would eagerly ask everyone who visited him about the nature of his illness and how long it would take to be well. He would feel highly consoled if he got a favourable answer. Again, like a child he

1. *Ibid.*, p.845.

would pull at the sleeve of the doctor and repeatedly implore him to cure him. He honoured the physicians belonging to all the systems of medicine. But if his own statements are any indication, he preferred the modern western system of medicine.

Sri Ramakrishna's Attitude Towards the Medical Profession

Personal likes and dislikes apart, how did Sri Ramakrishna look upon physicians in general? Some of his utterances convey the impression that he had a poor opinion about physicians. He has said, for example, on different occasions, 'I cannot eat the food offered by doctors and lawyers.'[1] 'It is difficult for a doctor, a broker, a lawyer to attain to true spirituality. How can the mind (of a doctor) preoccupied with the thought of mere medicine comprehend the Infinite?'[2] 'I haven't very much faith in your Calcutta physicians. When Sambhu became delirious, Dr. Sarvadhikari said,

---

1. Swami Gambhirananda, *Sri Ramakrishna Bhaktamalika*, Vol. II (Bengali), Udbodhan Karyalaya, Calcuttta, (1st ed.) p.290.

2. *Ibid.*, pp.163-64.

"Oh, it is nothing. It is grogginess from the medicine", and a little while after, Sambhu breathed his last.'[1]

The medical profession is considered one of the best professions. Writes Harrison: 'No greater opportunity, responsibility or obligation can fall to the lot of a human being than to become a physician. In the care of the suffering he needs technical skill, scientific knowledge and human understanding. He who uses these with courage, with humility, and with wisdom will provide a unique service for his fellow-men and will build an enduring edifice of character within himself. The physician should ask for his destiny no more than this; he should be content with no less.'[2]

Why was Sri Ramakrishna so critical of such a noble profession? This question was discussed by Latu Maharaj (Swami Adbhuta-nanda), a monastic disciple of Sri Ramakrishna, with three physician devotees.

---

1. *The Gospel*, p.386.

2. Harrison, T.R., Adams, R.D., Resnik, W.H., Thorn, G.W., and Winthrobe, M.M. - *Principles of Internal Medicine*, 1962, McGraw-Hill, New York, p.3.

Latu Maharaj (to the physicians): Can anyone hate your profession? How much good you do to patients! You save them from a lot of suffering. He (Sri Ramakrishna) used to say, 'Now indigenous drugs don't work. Now fever mixture is needed.'

One of the physicians: But he also said that doctors earn money by examining stool and urine. We have heard that he could not eat food offered by physicians.

Latu Maharaj: Listen! Consider why he said so. Ram Babu (Dr. Ramchandra Dutta) was a miser in his youth. To cure him of his stinginess he one day told him this. So Ram Babu thought it was useless to earn and hoard money if it could not be used in the service of his Guru. He asked Sri Ramakrishna what he should do. The Master said, "Serve the devotees. That would amount to serving me." He used to accept things offered by Ram Babu, and even ate the food brought by him. He spoke in that way so that Ram Babu might not have attachment for money. He never spoke out of hatred towards anybody.[1]

---

1. *Sri Sri Latu Maharajer Smrithi Katha* (Bengali) Udbodhan Karyalaya, II Edition, p.431-32.

Sri Ramakrishna himself has explained his attitude towards the medical profession thus: "Many think that the duty of a physician is a very noble one. The physician is undoubtedly a noble man if he treats his patients free, out of compassion and moved by their suffering. Then his work may be called very uplifting. But a physician becomes cruel and callous if he carries on his profession for money. It is very mean to do such things as examine urine and stool in order to earn money, like the business man carrying on his trade." "But the medical profession is certainly very noble if the physician devotes himself to the welfare of others in an unselfish spirit."[1]

Every profession is liable to abuse and corruption, and nobler the profession, greater are the possibilities of its degradation. For example, earning money with a certain amount of profit is an integral part of trade and commerce, and is not considered bad. But in medical profession asking money for one's services cannot

1. *The Gospel*, p.883.

be considered an ethical norm. According to medical ethics in ancient India, a physician was not supposed to demand fees. Even in the present age of general moral degradation, physicians are not wanting who never ask a fee, and accept whatever is offered willingly and who even spend from their own pocket, if need be, to treat their poor patients. As has been pointed out, the aim of the profession must be service to humanity and building of character, and if done with the spirit if dedication and humility, seeing God Himself in the patient as preached by Swami Vivekananda, this profession can become one of the highest form of spiritual practice.

Physicians in the Teachings of Sri Ramakrishna

Physicians have figured in several teachings of Sri Ramakrishna. While most of these teachings are of general interest and the illustrations of physicians have been used to explain spiritual truths, they have a special significance for the physicians who, by following them, can become better physicians.

Sri Ramakrishna divided physicians into three classes: "Superior, mediocre and inferior. The inferior physician feels the patient's pulse, merely asks him to take medicine and then goes away. He does not bother to find out whether the patient has followed his directions. The mediocre physician gently tries to persuade the patient to take the medicine. He says, 'Look here. How can you get well without medicine? Take the medicine, my dear. I am preparing it with my own hands.' But the superior physician follows a different method. If he finds the patient stubbornly refusing to swallow the medicine, he presses the patient's chest with his knee and forces the medicine down his throat." "There is no fear if a good physician presses the patient's chest with his knee."[1]

While this illustration has been given to explain the three classes of religious teachers, physicians will do well to take greater interest in the welfare of the patient. Such an approach has become imperative in present times when human relationships

_____

1. *Ibid.*, p.885-86.

in general are becoming more and more formal and superficial.

Everything depends upon the will of God. This applies, like everything else, to health, disease and death also. Says Sri Ramakrishna, "God laughs on two occasions. He laughs when two brothers divide land between them. ... God laughs again when the physician says to the mother weeping bitterly because of her child's desperate illness, 'Don't be afraid, mother, I shall cure your child.' The physician does not know that no one can save the child if God wills that he should die."[1] Miraculous cures in patients pronounced as hopeless and incurable, and sudden deaths in apparently healthy individuals are not uncommon experiences in every physician's professional career. "O Mother, all is done after Thine own sweet will...Thou workest Thine own work; men only call it theirs." None can appreciate this truth better than an humble, thoughtful physician.

Renunciation of the world is essential for those who would be the teachers of men.

---

1. *Ibid., p.323-24.*

To convey this truth, Sri Ramakrishna used to narrate the story of a physician who removed the jars of molasses from his room before asking the patient not to eat molasses.[1] Although it is not essential for physicians to practise what they preach, they would be able to elicit greater compliance to health rules from their patients if they themselves followed them.

Physicians' Opinion About Sri Ramakrishna

Apart from the physicians who recognised Sri Ramakrishna's spiritual excellence and accepted him as their spiritual guide or Guru, most of the other physicians were impressed by his childlike simplicity, absolute reliance on the physician and his gentlemanliness. Dr. Mahendralal Sarkar was so charmed by the human aspect of Sri Ramakrishna's personality that he sincerely believed that devotees were 'spoiling' such a guileless person by touching his feet and addressing him as an incarnation!

---

1. *Ibid.,* p.580.

What did the physicians think of Sri Ramakrishna's spiritual states and their effects as manifested in his body? As has been told earlier, some physicians had seen him during his period of Sadhana when he used to get excruciating burning sensation in the body. Some others had witnessed his ecstatic dance, and a rare few were fortunate enough to examine him during Samadhi and to find all the vital functions suspended. Sri Ramakrishna himself was keen to know the expert opinion of medical scientists regarding the physiological changes produced in him. For instance, he had asked Dr. Bhagwan Rudra what he thought of the twisting of his hand and stopping of the breath when he touched a coin. He actually demonstrated this to the doctor by holding a coin in his hand.

The first reaction of most physicians was that of amazement. Some Ayurvedic specialists tried to find an explanation of his 'malady' with the help of their science, but failed. One of them recognised it to be due to Yoga. Dr. Rudra thought it was due to the action of nerves. But none of the physicians was able to explain clearly the physiological phenomenon as manifested in Sri Ramakrishna.[1]

The least wish arising in the pure mind of a prophet of Sri Ramakrishna's eminence can never remain unfulfilled. Motivated by the silent wish of Sri Ramakrishna to know the physiological process behind the changes occurring in his body, lot of researches are being carried out in modern times in the field of neuro psychology. Although some experiments have been conducted on Yogis, the results are still inconclusive and the physiology of spiritual practices continues to remain a mystery.[2]

None of the utterances and actions of an incarnation are insignificant. Even though Sri Ramakrishna's relationship with physicians was short, and his sayings about them few, they have great significance for physicians as well as patients, who can enrich their life by the lessons derived from them.

---

1. *cf.* Shah, Dr. C.S., *Physiology of a Man of God,* The Vedanta Kesari, May, June, August, 1999.
2. *cf.* Chapter 13.

The Doctor–Patient Relationship

*N*o greater opportunity, responsibility or obligation can fall to the lot of a human being than to become a physician. In the care of the suffering he needs technical skill, scientific knowledge and human understanding. He who uses these with courage, with humility, and with wisdom will provide a unique service for his fellow-men and will build an enduring edifice of character within himself. The physician should ask for his destiny no more than this; he should be content with no less." (Harrison, 1962).

A medical student, a physician in the making, is taught technical skill and imparted scientific knowledge, but human understanding and the practice of humility which form an essential aspect of his profession are not taught to him any time during his period of training. And rightly so, because it is a virtue to be developed by the physician himself, with the guidance of those who have practised it throughout their life. It is precisely this vital and much neglected aspect of medical practice that is sought to be stressed in this brief article.

When, after passing the 1st M.B.B.S. examination, the medical student is sent to the wards of a hospital, he, for the first time, faces the suffering humanity. It is from this time on, that he should endeavour to develop the noble qualities of a physician as a healer. A sympathetic and discerning history-taking provides the first and the most important step. An unhurried interrogator, who listens to the tale of the sick patient sympathetically and patiently, will soon establish a relationship which not only can be utilised for investigations into the delicate aspect of family and personal history including matrimony but can also ripen from mere acquaintance to friendship.

Abdul Latif, a hopeless case of heart disease with double mitral lesion with cardiac failure was allotted to me when I first entered the wards while in the third year class. At the very first meeting he bluntly refused to talk to me. Nevertheless I persisted not in taking the history but daily talking to him on matters other than his illness; matters which interested him. I did not get annoyed with him and did not have enough confidence to scold him. But within four days he had developed enough confidence in me, and I, once having been able to cross over the first hurdle, proceeded to record a detailed history, did a complete examination and carried out painful investigations. Ultimately we became friends, so much so that every day he would be waiting for me and would insist on being examined by me daily. I, on my part, visited him daily even after my posting was changed. The story told to me by his fellow patients being, "Doctor, when you come, he smiles and talks, otherwise he remains sad and quiet throughout the day. He does not talk to anyone except you."

To be able to gain the confidence of the patient, two things must be remembered. First, that he is primarily a human being and next, a patient. It is necessary to view the patient more deeply as a complex organism with a vast repository of past experience and possessing a psyche which is subject to the effects of the environment. Secondly, illness constitutes a threat not only to the physical integrity of the individual but also to his status in his social group. By the time a patient comes to the physician, he is ill not only in his body but is also sick in his mind with apprehension and discouragement, anxiety and depression. Thus the physician must keep in mind the social and economic implications of the patient's illness. Along with the body he should endeavour to treat the mind as well.

A simple method of developing human understanding is to imagine oneself in place of the patient. For example, imagine yourself to be a middle class person with a large family and an income just enough to meet the bare necessities of life. You fall ill and have to lie down in the hospital for about a month. Imagine the plight of your family. Imagine your worry about carrying the children to school, future of the eldest daughter, care of the aged father, money for the medicine, danger of losing the job or losing the pay at least! Thus, cultivating the capacity to see deeply and understandingly into the problems of another human being is the first step.

During interview with the patient, the physician often finds it difficult to control his own reaction of disinterestedness, irritation, annoyance and hateful repulsion. Disinterest because the patient presents no fascinating problem of organic disease; irritation at his verbosity, lack of consistency and clarity in history; annoyance because the illness fails to respond to treatment in the expected manner; repulsion because of lack of cleanliness, culture, and lack of intelligent cooperation on the part of the patient. The physician can hardly expect to achieve a deep appreciation or gain confidence of the patient unless he controls himself. Thus the second step is to learn to control one's own emotional reactions.

The above lesson, I learnt while observing one of my senior and much respected doctor friend. A mentally abnormal and much talkative patient, rebuked, insulted and unattended by all, approached him, and this physician gave a very sympathetic and patient hearing to all his curt and meaningless talk. This considerate behaviour had such an effect on the patient that while leaving, he complimented him thus, "Doctor, you are the only person who is sympathetic to me. I am fully satisfied. Now even if you don't treat me I would not mind." Perhaps, this feeling of lack of affection was the only cause of his ailment, or, may be, it was the cause of his altered mental state. At times, the physician also comes across an intelligent patient, who may not only provide a precise history, but may also go to the extent of suggesting the diagnosis and line of treatment. Neither should the physician assume all that to be correct which his patient may suggest nor should he disregard an unimportant complaint of an illiterate patient. "The sufferer, i.e., the patient is never wrong." This is a practical and safe rule, for the patient as well as for the doctor.

The third means of keeping the patient in confidence is to keep him cheered up. Humour is one of the most important factors in the development of the doctor-patient relationship. But it is rarely mentioned or pointed out to the young doctor. It not only relieves the anxious patient but also relaxes the worried doctor. Monotonous dry re-assurances are, most of the time, of little value, and indeed may even be harmful, but a light touch, like a wry comment on the absurdities of the medical procedures may lift many a cloud of depression and anxiety from over the patient and leave him smiling. It is an excellent rule to approach the patient cracking jokes or telling stories, and thus creating a relaxed atmosphere. If the doctor appears to take the symptoms seriously, the patient would imagine that he was more ill than he really was. (It is equally important, however, to remember exceptions to this rule.)

Lastly, the physician should bring to the suffering patient a sense of security. He should be convinced that all that is possible would be done for him, not only by words but also by deeds. The patient must feel that his unique individuality is recognised and appreciated, and his life's problems are considered meaningful.

I have already pointed out the advantage of a successful doctor-patient communication, which I would summarise now. Osler quotes Galen as saying: "He cures most successfully in whom people have the greatest confidence." (Cecil and Loeb, 1959). No proof of this is needed as even quacks are known to treat successfully. And how does this occur? Compassion and warmth of behaviour break down the barriers of anxiety and fear, and make the patient more cooperative for unpleasant diagnostic and therapeutic procedures. In fact, it makes the whole process more pleasant.

"The physician should never think that the practice of medicine yields no benefit to him. Sometimes he may get money, sometimes he may get what he desires; occasionally he may win fame or friendship. Even when he does not obtain any of these, there is bound to be at least the benefit of practical experience."

Most of the students who aspire to be admitted to the medical colleges are interested primarily because of the bright financial prospects which the profession offers. It is true that a high percentage of doctors are very well off. But it also is a fact that patients flock round those physicians who are polite, sympathetic and considerate, and no one likes to go to an irritable and short tempered doctor.

A galaxy of doctors have made name and gained fame, the most outstanding amongst them was Dr. Albert Schwitzer. He was awarded Nobel prize for his humanitarian work in the dark forests of Africa. Famous men in other spheres are soon forgotten, but a patient who has been relieved of his agony by a compassionate doctor never forgets his benefactor for the rest of his life, specially if the doctor had renounced the financial gains he could have otherwise derived from this patient.

Much can be gained at times in the intellectual sphere. Quite a number of patients are persons with a high intellectual acumen and once their confidence is gained, they might provide a store of useful information and knowledge in their spheres of activity. A mutual interest in various arts, culture, history and even politics between the two can lead to an interchange of useful views. The physician should not hesitate in extracting this justified advantage of his superior position in relation to the patient.

But as has been pointed out in the beginning of this article, the most significant gain of combining intelligently technical skill with humility and human understanding is the building up of a noble character. "Money does not pay, nor name; fame does not pay, nor learning; it is love that pays; it is character that cleaves its way through adamantine walls of difficulties."

Blessed indeed is a physician who has been provided with a golden opportunity to serve the Lord in the shape of the diseased, in the shape of the poor, in the shape of the suffering.

The ultimate aim of all the dealings of a physician with the patient should be to please God—and to serve the Almighty. This form of service will take him to the highest perfection of mankind. Here is an opportunity for him to enter the 'Kingdom of Heaven' and let him fully avail of this opportunity.

Medical Ethics in Ancient India

$\mathscr{S}$ince time immemorial, in India, the rules and regulations for different social groups and the code of conduct for people belonging to various professions were framed in such a way as to lead them to the highest spiritual culmination of their life. It is in accordance with the teaching of the *Bhagavad Gita* (18.45) that each individual can attain a high state of perfection by rightly following his duty or *Svadharma*. The medical profession was no exception in this respect. Although its immediate aim was the alleviation of physical and mental suffering, its ultimate aim was to help the patient, the nurse and the physician to attain everlasting happiness and bliss.

It is very likely that *Ayurveda*, the ancient Indian medical science, evolved out of religion. Historians are of the view that in remote past the only therapy available for ailments was spiritual—so called *Daiva Vyapasraya cikitsa*,[1] comprising procedures and acts such as reciting incantations, chanting of hymns, keeping talismans, wearing gems, observance of vows and making atonements, offering gifts and donations, propitiating deities by offerings, going on pilgrimages, etc. Such acts are in vogue even today since psychic disorders are often seen to improve by them, and the persons performing them gain in physical and mental health. It is, therefore, natural that many of the religious values and moral codes would form part and parcel of the medical ethics in ancient times as well. In Ayurvedic texts one finds wholesome and ample instructions for a healthy and pious mode of life.

Definition of Ethics

Ethics is the science of moral values. Medical ethics consists of the moral principles which should guide members of the medical profession in their dealings with

---

1. Jyotir Mishra, *'Religion and Medicine'*, Lecture delivered at the 17th Biennial function of Ayurveda, Vijayawada, Andhra Pradesh.

each other, with their patients and with society and the state.

In ancient Indian literature the word used for ethics was *sadvrtta*,[1] which etymologically means, 'the right physical, mental and vocal conduct expected of the pious.' Caraka, the father of Indian medicine, advises everyone desiring peace and happiness to observe the rules of right conduct diligently. He who follows the ethical code gains mastery over the senses and obtains a healthy body.[2] He authoritatively advocates ethics as a part of personal hygiene. Vagbhatta, too, claims that man can attain long and healthy life, wealth and fame in this existence, and glory and higher spheres after death by following the ethical code.[3]

The ancient sages framed the rules of ethics and built up early Indian society in such a way that character could be moulded from the very childhood and the

1. Commentary of Chakrapani on *Caraka Samhita*, *Sutra Sthana*, 8:17. Choukhamba Sanskrit Samsthana, Varanasi, U.P. 1984.

2. *Caraka Samhita*, Sutra 8:17-18.

3. Vagbhatta, *Astanga Hridaya*, Sutra 2:48. New Delhi: Motilal Banarasidass, 1990.

individual could grow into a useful citizen. The ethical training began at home with the parents, was extended to the schools through the teachers, and continued in professional life later with the help of the wise and leaders of society.

The Aim of Indian Medicine

Although as a profession the medical practice provides a livelihood for the physician, the wise have condemned its being for that purpose only. Those who would sell their skills to make a business out of the practice of medicine are like persons who would pursue a heap of dust, as it were, letting go a mass of gold.[1] Medicine must be practised neither for wealth nor for fulfillment of worldly desires, but only out of compassion for creatures.[2] There is no austerity higher than treating the sick. It leads to destruction of sins, accumulation of virtue, and benefits both here and hereafter.[3]

---

1. *Caraka*, op. cit., 1.56.

2. *Ibid.*, 1.58.

3. *Kalyana Karaka*, 7:32; Sakharam Nemichand Granthamala, Solapur, 1940.

The physician must not undertake treatment of a patient motivated by his own love, lust or greed. Nor even friendship, enmity or affection for a kinsman should be a reason for giving his treatment. The expectation of earning a reward, or the acquisition of fame too, should not tempt the physician. Only one urge and aim–that is, kindness and mercy, should prompt the physician to practise the art of healing.[1]

The practice of medicine is never fruitless. Sometimes a physician may earn money. Sometimes he may get what he desires. Occasionally he may win fame or friendship. But even if he does not obtain any of these, there is bound to come to him, at least, the benefit of practical experience.[2] As long as the earth is inhabited by human beings who cannot remain completely free from illness and disease, the physician need never worry about unemployment or starvation.[3] The gifts of life and health are the highest among duties. Those benefited

---

1. *Ibid.*, 7:33-34.
2. *Ibid.*, 7:36.
3. *Ibid.*, 7:37.

by such gifts may, out of gratitude, either praise the physician or pay him with due renumeration. In this way his needs of *Dharma* (duty), *artha* (money), and *kama* (desire) are fulfilled.[1]

An individual can be happy or unhappy personally and harmful or helpful to society. The ancient seers not only set the above mentioned high aims and ideals before the individual, but framed the ethical code in such a way that the physician could both derive the maximum benefit from the pursuit of his profession and prove helpful, not harmful, to society. Thus the final aim of the ethical code was the attainment of harmony and equilibrium at all the three levels, physical, mental and social.[2]

Qualities of a Good Physician

According to Susruta, the great ancient Indian surgeon, a medical graduate must

---

1. *Kasyapa*, quoted by Sharma Gaur, Pt. Damodar, in Medical Ethics in Ayurveda, *Sacitra Ayurveda*, June 1962, p.1032.

2. *Caraka*, op. cit., 1:41.

meet the following standards for starting his practice. He must have learnt and mastered both the theory and practice of the art of healing, and must have obtained permission from the governing authority. He must wear clean white dress, which should not be ostentatious. He must remain clean shaven and tie his hair in a knot. He must be cheerful, noble, large hearted, well behaved, polite and friendly towards all creatures.[1] While walking along the road he should proceed forward looking ahead, far and wide. On meeting others he must accost them first. He must always speak clearly without ambiguity and doubts, sweetly and ingenuously in a simple and ethical tone, avoiding controversies, and in accordance with the law of *dharma*.[2]

Kalyana Karaka lays down further qualifications of a physician. He must be a speaker of truth, a man of courage, endowed with patience, blessed with a lucky hand

---

1. *Susruta Samhita, Sutrasthana*, 10:3. Choukhamba Orientalia, Varanasi, 1980.

2. Subba Reddi, D.V., '*Medical Ethics in Ancient India*', *J. Indian Medical Association*, Vol. 37, No. 6, 1961, p. 287.

that has achieved many cures, one who has witnessed and practised notable methods of treatment, and one who does not get upset under any adverse circumstances.[1] Caraka advises the physician to carefully assess his ability to treat a particular case before taking it up.[2] This precaution is important, specially in the beginning of the career of the fresh graduate, not only for the patient, but also for the reputation of the physician.

According to Caraka, vast knowledge of medicine, extensive practical experience, dexterity and purity are the four qualifications of a physician.[3] A reputation as unfailing in prescribing appropriate medicines is another qualification. One who possesses the fourfold knowledge regarding cause, diagnosis, cure and prevention of diseases is fit to be appointed a royal physician.[4] The effectiveness of medical knowledge (like any instrument or weapon) to a large

---

1. *Kalyana Karaka*, op. cit., 7.38.
2. *Caraka*, op. cit., 8.86.
3. *Ibid.*, 9.6.
4. *Ibid.*, 9.19.

extent depends upon the person who handles it. Hence the physician must always continue to sharpen his intellect and increase his proficiency.[1] Elsewhere Caraka enumerates six qualities of a successful physician as follows: Having knowledge, critical approach, insight into allied sciences, sharp memory, promptness and perseverance. To these he adds sharp intellect, practical experience, continued practice, success in treatment, and being in consultation with an experienced teacher.[2]

Since there is no limit to knowledge, Caraka advises the physician to try to learn every moment. According to Susruta, study, discussion, perusal of foreign literature and devoted service to the masters of particular techniques are essential for gaining wider knowledge and improving skills. One cannot come to the right conclusion by studying just one aspect of a subject. Hence the physician must learn other viewpoints also to become proficient.[3]

---

1. *Ibid.*, 9.20.
2. *Ibid.*, 9.21-22.
3. *Susruta Samhita*, 4:7.

Code of Conduct While Treating the Sick

A Physician must not visit a patient at his residence uninvited and without prior intimation. On being invited he must go to the house of the patient and observe the portents and signs. He must not look at anyone other than the patient, and all his senses must be alert and concentrated on him. Every action of the physician should be precise and deliberate.[1]

The physician must not converse or make fun with the ladies of the patient's house-hold, nor should he refer to their names disrespectfully. He should not sit with them in private, nor show excessive regard towards them.

A physician must not reveal the secrets of the household or the patient, nor spread broadcast the demerits of the family. A patient may not have faith in his father, mother, friend or children but may open his heart to the physician. He must therefore never expose the patient and must honour the confidence the patient has in him.[2]

---

1. *Kasyapa Samhita. Vimanasthan, 1:8.*
2. *Susruta Samhita, Sutrasthana, 25:43-44.*

A definite order must be followed while treating a patient. First, the physician must examine the patient throughly before arriving at a diagnosis. Next he must decide the treatment and lay down the course of management.[1] Vagbhatta warns the physician against starting treatment without complete knowledge of a case, which could be responsible for the loss of art, fame, reputation or whatever other benefit the patient and physician may have derived.[2]

After initiating his treatment, the physician should observe the progress of the disease and the condition of the patient at frequent intervals, and should modify his treatment accordingly.[3] The rules and the order of prescribing medicines as laid down in the scriptures must be followed. Medicines of one's own invention must not be prescribed.[4]

If the condition of the patient deteriorates or serious complications arise, he

---

1. *Caraka,* op. cit., 20.20.
2. Vagbhatta, *Astanga Sangraha, Sutrasthana,* 2:31.
3. *Caraka,* op. cit., 8:37.
4. *Kasyapa Samahita,* op. cit., 9:8

must not be told directly. Nor should the relatives of the patient be told directly about the impending death, which may badly shock them. Instead, the physician may indirectly hint at the prognosis thus: "None is immortal in this transitory world, nor can one escape death. However, disease can be cured and suffering can be alleviated"[1] Or, "The physician is not the master of life. He is the knower of diseases and the reliever of suffering."[2]

During emergencies, every available means must be employed with minimum loss of time. If the life of the patient is threatened the physician must inform the relatives and friends of the patient and start his treatment after obtaining their consent.[3]

General Rules of Social Conduct

With a view that a physician should be an ideal citizen, numerous rules of

---

1. *Ibid.*

2. *Bhaishajya Ratnavali,* 3:15; Chaukhamba Sanskrit Sansthana, 1896.

3. (a) *Vagbhatta, Sutrasthana,* 23.

   (b) *Caraka Samhita,* 13:176.

conduct have been laid down for him in the ancient literature.

The physician should never harbour ill will towards fellow physicians or get into confronatations with them. If need be, he may join them in treating a case and should not hesitate to consult them in deciding the diagnosis and treatment of a case. He must pardon the unethical conduct of his colleague, or politely try to set him right. But if the envious opponent continues to criticize his procedure, he must defeat him by his knowledge and experience. Even while defending himself the physician must avoid harsh words and use ethical language. He must always be suggestive and never direct.[1]

Advertisement or self-aggrandizement by a physician was poorly esteemed in ancient India. Self-praise is not only unpleasant to others, it is disagreeable also to a really deserving but dignified physician.[2] With a view to decrying such boastful physicians Caraka gives a picturesque

---

1. *Kaśyapa Samhita* op. cit., 1.9.
2. *Caraka* op. cit., 8:13

description of how such egoistic fellows engage in broadcasting their own virtues and abusing others.[1]

A physician is entitled to due remuneration for his services, and it is enjoined that none should go to a physician empty-handed.[2] According to Caraka, anyone who does not repay the help obtained from physician remains under an eternal debt.[3] On his part, the physician must treat Brahmins, preceptors, the poor, friends, wandering monks, orphans, and other such people in need, gratuitously.[4]

The physician must not attempt treatment of a patient whose death is certain or who has an incurable disease, or if he has not the necessary facilities for treatment.[5] Often, in ancient India, charitable physicians supplied medicines to poor patients who could not afford them. Although it appears inhuman to deny

---

1. *Ibid.*, 29:9.
2. *Bhava Prakasa*, 5:52.
3. *Caraka*, 1.55.
4. *Susruta Samhita*, 2:8.
5. Subba Reddy, P. 187.

help to anyone seeking it, there were certain restrictions on physicians in ancient society. Caraka, for example, advises physicians not to treat enemies of the state or the rulers. The list of persons debarred includes the mentally abnormal, the wicked, people of blemished character and conduct, those who had not vindicated their honour, and those who had no guardians, especially women.[1]

Apart from voluntary gifts from patients, physicians were paid by the state according to their merit and efficiency. They were liable to punishment if they committed mistakes or indulged in unethical practices, the severity of the punishment varying with the seriousness of the offence.[2] Caraka also describes the malpractices of quacks and decries them in uncompromising terms. He considers them murderers in the guise of physicians, who introduce and spread diseases rather than curing them. They flourished because the government failed to curb them.[3]

1. *Caraka* 8:13.
2. *Kautilya, Arthasastram,* 4:1, 56-57.
3. *Caraka,* 29:8.

Summary

It will be noticed that the above rules of moral conduct culled from various sources, aimed at making a physician not only a perfect physician but a perfect human being. Vagbhatta has briefly summarized the qualities of an ideal physician as follows: A physician must be steadfast, dignified, patient, truthful, good looking, well-read, master of his subject, and a knower of the effect of time. He should honour the teachers and treat the orphans and the sick as his children. He must visit the patient only when invited and with pure intentions. In the patient's house, he must pay attention only to the patient and to nothing else. He must thoroughly examine the patient, arrive at a diagnosis and plan the line of treatment. He must not disclose the secrets of the patient, must not waste time during emergency and must be capable of handling serious and urgent cases.[1]

A physician was to be friendly to all, compassionate towards the suffering,

---

11. *Vagbhatta, Sutrasthana,* 2.

pleased with the healthy, and indifferent towards the wicked.[1]

Qualities of the Nurses and Attendants

According to ancient Indian medicine, the patient, physician, medicine and nurse are the four limbs of medical treatment.[2] The ideal condition for each of these four limbs to contribute the maximum are described in the ancient medical Literature. We have already seen the qualities of a physician.

According to Caraka, purity, efficiency, having the knowledge of the art of nursing, and devotion to the physician, are the four cardinal qualities of a good nurse.[3] According to another text the nurse and attendant of the patient must be strong, fore-bearing and forgiving, desirous of doing good to others, efficient, polite, and well behaved.[4] He or she must be of clean habits, good-natured, kind-hearted, and

1. *Ibid., Uttarasthana.* 50.
2. *Caraka,* 9:23.
3. *Ibid.,* 9.8.
4. *Kalyana Karaka,* 7:41.

proficient in other kinds of work, like cooking, sponging and bathing the patient, preparing and administering medicines, ambulating patients and carrying goods from one place to another. Attendants and nurses must not be grumblers, and must be willing to do all kinds of work.[1] Caraka is of the opinion that women nurses, especially those who are mothers of many children, are best suited to become nurses because of their constant, kind, and gentle manner. They have better understanding of patients, are hard working, patient, forebearing and able to stand excessive strain. Their common sense and presence of mind specially qualifies them for nursing difficult patients.[2]

Characteristics of An Ideal Patient

The third limb of medical treatment is the patient himself. It is needless to say that the treatment of a cooperative, intelligent patient is much easier, and considerably helps to improve the prognosis. According

---

1. *Ibid.*, 15.7.
2. *Caraka,* 8:34.

to Caraka, a good memory, willingness to follow the instructions of the physician, fearlessness, and not hiding any relevant information about his symptoms and disease are the four qualities of a good patient.[1] He further states that one who takes a wholesome diet, who possesses healthy physical habits, who acts after giving thought and consideration, who is unattached to objects of sense enjoyment, who is charitable, truthful, same-sighted, forgiving and who serves the learned, seldom falls ill.[2] Disease rarely strikes a person who leads an austere life, has a habit of meditation, and who engages himself in higher intellectual pursuits.[3]

Caraka gives a long list of virtues which must be cultivated if one wishes to remain free from psychosomatic disorders. One must perform religious duties, be friendly towards all, pacify the angry, reassure the frightened, and be compassionate towards the poor and miserable. One must be able

---

1. *Ibid.*, 9.7.
2. *Ibid.*, 2:46
3. *Ibid.*, 2:47.

to make compromises, and be forbearing of unpleasant words of others. One must have a peaceful disposition and root out hatred and attachment from oneself. One must not be driven helplessly by a restless mind, nor become a slave to inordinate appetites of the senses. One must never act in a fit of anger or become over-elated or submerged in grief. One should neither become conceited in success nor be depressed in failure.[1] The *Samhita* is replete with such instructions meant to foster the cultivation of charity, chastity, friendship, compassion, detachment and peace.[2]

Apart from the general ethical admonitions, Caraka gives detailed instructions about food, clothing, exercise, sleep, sex, relationship with women, and the like, which need not be elaborated here. Suffice to state that in ancient India, physical and mental health were never considered separate from sane living.[3]

---

1. *Ibid.*, 8.27.
2. *Ibid.*, 8:29.
3. *Ibid.*, 8:17-28.

Conclusion

Each country has its own code of ethics. In India, where there are several systems of medicine practised, there are various ethical codes governing the members who practise under these different systems. Nevertheless, there are many principles common to them in the ancient medical ethics, as there are among the various codes of modern medical ethics. There are some important differences too.

The four cardinal aims set before the doctor are: preservation of life, curing of illness and lessening of suffering, prevention of diseases, and the advancement of knowledge. As has been elaborated, the aims set before the physicians in ancient India, while including the above four aims, were far wider, loftier and nobler. They were no less than the spiritual emancipation and eternal happiness of the patient, the nurse and the doctor, and the building up of a sane society.

It must be noted that the ethical principles and moral admonitions are incorporated into, and form part and parcel of, the body of such authoritative ancient medical texts as the *Caraka Samhita,* the *Susruta Samhita,* and others. In contrast, most of the texts of modern medicine are totally devoid of ethical instruction. Nor does ethics form a part of the curriculum in modern medical education. The ancient system of incorporating ethics into medical education is worthy of adoption in modern times. This suggestion becomes all the more relevant in view of the fact that now a days there is seen a sharp decline in professional ethical behaviour. Let the modern medical men be reminded that "No greater opportunity, responsibility or obligation can fall to the lot of a human being than to become a physician. In the care of the suffering, he needs technical skill, scientific knowledge and human understanding. He who uses these with courage, with humility, and with wisdom, will provide a unique service for his fellow men and will build an enduring edifice of character within himself. The physician should ask for this destiny no more than this; he should be content with no less."[1]

1. Harrison et, all. *Principles of Internal Medicine,* 1962, p. 3.

Tranquillity and Tranquillizers

*W*e are living in war times. Although there has been no overt major war in the last four decades, few would claim that they enjoy real peace. The U.N.O. has been able to defer the dreaded 'Third World War' for almost half a century, but smaller wars have been and are still being fought all over the world. Fighting in Sri Lanka, Iraq-Iran, Libya, the spate of violence in the Punjab, and on the streets of major cities, dacoities and murders in villages, child abuse—the list of examples of human cruelty goes on and on. Indeed, so common are instances of violence and aggression that it is impossible to pick up a newspaper, leaf through a magazine or tune in the radio for news without learning of some frightening new atrocity. It seems that only the fear of total extermination of the human race from the face of earth has somehow prevented the 'Third War'. But it has been replaced by international terrorism, the latest form of war. War, which used to be fought in the bygone days on the battlefield away from towns and villages, has now come to the citizen's door steps. In desperation the U.N.O. had called for the observance of an International Year of Peace in 1986. This is symbolic of the distress of the world.

At the individual level the situation is no better. Although science and technology have made life easy, they have also multiplied human wants. While shaking man's faith in God and traditional values, science has not offered a better substitute. Consequently, life of man has become shallow and unsteady. The unprecedented expansion and proliferation of the media and means of communication have increased the input of information, but man has not learnt to manage or utilize it effectively. Competition at every level of life has increased hurry and worry and has contributed further to unrest. All these and many other factors have made man restless, nervous, tense and insecure.

Unrest at both these levels, international and individual, are inter-related. A restless agitated man disturbs his environment and in turn is influenced by the conflicts and struggles around him. Peace therefore must be sought at both these levels.

But what after all is peace? According to the Upanishads, *santam,* the peaceful, is one of the names of the formless, absolute Reality.[1] It is also described in many Sanskrit hymns[2] as one of the attributes of the Saguna Brahman, God with attributes. This Tranquil Ultimate in the absolute sense is the substratum and the matrix from which the manifest universe arises and on which it rests. This again is the substratum of all the mental disturbances a person may experience. To know, to experience and to become one with it is the ultimate solution of all the problems. Says Swami Vivekananda, "Waves may roll over the surface and tempest rage, but deep down

---

1. *Shantam Shivamadvaitam, Mandukya Upanishad,* 7.

2. *Shantam Shashvatamaprameyamanagham,* and *Shantakaram Bhujagashayanam,* etc.

there is the stratum of infinite calmness, infinite peace and infinite bliess."[1]

Yet the common man has always been seeking worldly pleasures and temporary satisfaction of desires. However, serious minded people of all races and times, having realized the impermanence of worldly objects, have sought permanent peace and satisfaction. More than three thousand years ago, Zarathustra (Zoroaster), the Persian prophet, had asked how man can attain a peaceful mind. Narada too had approached the ancient sage Sanatkumara to know the secret of peace,[2] because in spite of all his knowledge, he had not become free from sorrow. The same problem persists even today.

By tranquillity is not meant the peace of a stone or a wall. Nor is it the peace experienced in deep sleep, however refreshing, soothing or blissful. Worldly objects or achievements, however satisfying, are never permanent and are always fraught with fear

---

1. *The Complete Works of Swami Vivekananda*, Vol. IV, 1985, p.374.

2. *Chandogya Upanishad*, VII.1.3.

or loss.[1] "To the discriminating, everything is painful either as consequence, or as anticipation of loss of happiness, or as fresh craving arising from impressions of happiness and as contradiction of qualities or Gunas."[2] In deep sleep Tamas predominates. Craving for sense-enjoyments makes the mind restless and dominated by Rajas. In the tranquil Sattvika mind alone does the bliss of Atman shine forth. The mind becomes restless either by external stimuli or by desires and passions and by promptings of ego arising from within. Therefore, "He alone attains peace in whom all sense-objects enter even as rivers enter the ocean, which remains unaffected though being filled, and not one who is desirous of enjoyments. Giving up sense-objects, the person who goes about unattached, free from the idea of ownership and egoism, attains peace."[3]

To attain tranquillity, various means, ranging from sheer hedonism to extreme

---

1. Bhartrihari, *Vairagya Shatakam*, 31.
2. *Yoga Sutras*, 2.15.
3. *Gita*, 2.70-71.

asceticism, from prolonged arduous Yoga to instant-acting drugs, have been tried. Man has tried to insulate himself from external stimuli by withdrawing into solitude or by deliberately disregarding the disturbing facts of life. He has tried to suppress his desires and passions by imposing moral and ethical codes, but such attempts have only intensified his restlessness by creating subconscious tension. With no better results others have tried a free expression of their suppressed desires. Another method widely tried through the ages is the use of drugs.

The use of drugs to affect mental function has been in vogue since times immemorial. "All naturally occuring sedatives, narcotics, euphoriants, hallucinogens and excitants were discovered thousands of years ago before the dawn of civilization."[1] It is very unlikely that humanity will ever be able to dispense with artificial paradises awarded by drugs. "Most men and women lead lives at worst so painful and at best

---

1. Huxley, A (1957), *Ann. N. Y. Acad. Sci.* 67,677. (Quoted by Laurence D.R. and Bennett, P.N. in *Clinical Pharmacology*, (1982); ELBS and Churchill Livingstone, p.447).

so monotonous, poor and limited, that the urge to escape, the longing to transcend themselves, if only for a few moments, is and has always been one of the principal cravings of the soul."[1] On the contrary, the use of psychotropic drugs, i.e., drugs which alter the mood or the consciousness, is on the increase. The use of hallucinogens, narcotics and sedatives has become so prevalent in Western countries, and specially in U.S.A., that it has become a major health hazard.

The psychotropic drugs used for non-medical purpose are broadly classified into two groups:[2] Hard drugs and soft drugs. Drugs like heroin, morphine and its analogues which seriously disable an individual as a functioning member of the society by inducing severe emotional and physical dependence are called hard drugs. Here the drug is central in the user's life. Soft drugs are less dependence producing and their use is usually incidental. These

---

1. Huxley, A (1959) *The Doors of Perception,* (London: Chatto and Windus). Quoted by Laurence and Bennett, *op cit.* p.447.

2. Laurence and Bennett, *op cit.* p.448.

include sedatives, tranquillizers, amphetamines, hallucinogens, alcohol and tobacco. Among these the drugs that are supposed to bring about tranquillity by calming, soothing or pacifying the mind are called tranquillizers. These again are of two types: *(i) Major Tranquillers:* These are therapeutically effective in psychoses and cause emotional quietening and psychomotor slowing. *(ii) Minor Tranquillizers* or *Anxiolytic Sedatives:* These reduce pathological anxiety, tension and agitation, but do not have therapeutic effect in major disturbances of cognition and perception.

Apart from the use of major tranquillizers and other psychotropic drugs in mental diseases like schizophrenia, anxiety, depression, mania, etc. where they are used under medical supervision and prescription, many tranquillizers are used by the laity without a medical prescription, and on grounds not accepted medically. The dividing line between the legitimate use and abuse of psychotropic drugs for such non-medical and social purposes is not distinct, for it is not only a matter of the type of drug used but also the quantity consumed. For example, temperate use of tobacco, and in many European countries alcohol (a form of self-medication), to insulate from environmental stress and anxiety and to ease social intercourse is generally accepted as a norm. But given the appropriate degree of mental abnormality or environmental adversity, many may become dependent on them both emotionally and physically.

There are various motives for non-medical drug use. The tranquillizers are used for relief of anxiety, tension and depression and as an escape from personal psychological problems. Rebellion against or despair about the orthodox social values and environment may prompt others to take drugs. Some may use them in an attempt to achieve conformity with one's social subgroup and for fear of being lonely. Many, however, take drugs (not necessarily tranquillizers) for fun, amusement, excitement–'kick' as it is called–and out of curiosity. Hallucinogens and LSD are used in search of 'self knowledge' and 'spiritual' experience. They have also been used for aestheticism, to stimulate artistic creativity

and for attaining genuine, sincere interpersonal relationship.

Justification for the Use of Tranquillizers

It is never safe to use tranquillizers, or
for that matter any drug, without medical
advice. The hazards of tobacco and alcohol
are too well-known to need re-statement.
The use of narcotics and hard drugs has
been legally banned. Yet the question
remains whether soft drugs can be used
judiciously to solve at least some of the
mental problems of modern man, beset
as he is with stress and strain of the type
unknown and never experienced in the past?
Can they help bring about social harmony
by blunting the emotional reaction of individuals? Can they be used to obtain psychic
experiences and thus impart depth and
purpose to the otherwise shallow, aimless
life of man? Finally, can they make man more
spiritual or accelerate the process of human
development and evolution?

Stress, both physical and mental, is an
inseparable part of human existence. Man
is subject to disease, loss and death. Even
growth from childhood into adulthood

involves leaving the care of parents and facing newer challenges. Events so serious as death of a spouse to so trivial as receiving guests or changing eating habits may involve stress of change. The individual responds to such situations by anxiety and arousal. Anxiety and arousal therefore play a very useful part in the survival, growth, and evolution of the organism. An imagined or real sense of inability to cope with the situation causes depression. Anxiety based on real danger in the external world is called 'reality-anxiety'. But excessive anxiety, i.e., more than the optimum, reduces efficiency of the individual in satisfying his needs and disturbs his interpersonal relationship. Severe anxiety serves no useful purpose. Instead it produces confusion and impedes performance. It is in these cases of excessive anxiety that the anxiolytic tranquillizers may prove useful when used temporarily as long as the stressful situation persists. They are also useful in the prevention and treatment of those psychosomatic diseases where anxiety plays a major etiological role.

There is another type of anxiety (and depression) called neurotic or endogenous in which anxiety is not based on the objective appraisal of the external situation but springs from imagined threats. This has its roots in the predisposing personality of the individual and cannot be cured by drugs alone. Prolonged regular use of tranquillizers in such cases is liable to produce psychological dependence. Moreover, most drugs have harmful side effects. They can cause undue sedation, impair memory and reduce mental efficiency of the user. They may hinder the function of vital organs or may even damage them. Tobacco is known to produce coronary artery disease, peptic ulcer, cancer and bronchitis. There is good reason to believe that efficiency, both mental and physical, is reduced by alcohol taken in any quantity even for social purposes.

That drugs or chemicals can impart psychic experience and mental powers (Siddhis) was known in India since ancient times. Although Patanjali, the father of Yoga, has recognized this fact,[1] he does not give importance to it in his system. The drugs

---

11. *Yoga Sutras*, 4.1.

which affect cerebral function in such a way as to produce a psychic experience are called psycho-dysleptics or hallucinogens. Marijuana (Cannabis) and LSD are the two best known, the former as milder and the latter as stronger members of the group. They alter time sense, make sensations more vivid and obstruct memory revival. There may be a feeling of deep insight; hence these drugs are also called 'mind-manifesting'. Cannabis may accentuate a particular mood or facilitate a train of thought and action which could explain the increased criminality associated with it. This is also accompanied by a feeling of unease and a sense of ineffectiveness leading to lethargy and social passivity.

The effect of LSD is more dramatic but less predictable. It may produce a feeling of supreme happiness or of fear and depression. Both these drugs reduce mental problem-solving capacity. In spite of their wide use and in spite of the voluminous literature on the subject, it is uncertain whether these drugs can produce a true mystic experience. They do not induce an experience but may facilitate it in susceptible individuals. There is not enough evidence that the experience so produced can stimulate or accelerate the process of spiritual development, alter the character of the user for the better or make him more human or altruistic. Indeed, reliance on repeated drug experience may inhibit the development of independence which is vital for the freedom of the spirit and true spirituality. Since these drugs do not serve any socio-ethical purpose and since they may increase criminal tendency or badly disturb the user, they have been put under legal control. They may be useful in applied and experimental psychiatry.

Tranquillity and Tranquillizers

It is true that tranquillizers can impart tranquillity, but the shallow temporary tranquillity produced by drugs cannot be compared to, nor should be confused with, the lasting profound peace of spiritual realization. Tranquillizers merely quieten the superficial mental disturbances but do not solve the deeper psychological conflicts. Nor do they help conquer the desires and passions, which are the real cause of unrest.

It is also true that some drugs can stir up the subconscious mind and bring to surface hidden conflicts and complexes, but it is uncertain whether the experience so produced can be classed as a true mystic experience. Needless to say, the direct experience of the Supreme Reality in its personal or impersonal aspect, the "stratum of infinite peace", is impossible with the help of drugs.

Finally, it is also true that by prolonged use some drugs can alter the character and conduct of the user. But this change is never for the better. They tend to increase Tamas, rather than Sattva. They cannot turn a man into a god but can certainly bring the devil out of him. They are incapable of making a saint but are potent enough to produce a sinner.

Tranquillizers and other psychotropic drugs have a very limited scope so far as imparting deep and lasting peace is concerned. The major drugs are useful in the treatment of established mental disorders. Moderate and occasional use of 'soft' drugs and minor tranquillizers may be accepted in the modern social structure for relaxation and for protection and relief from anxiety and depression for those whose sole aim is a decent social living. For a sincere spiritual aspirant seeking ultimate peace and determined to bear the physical and mental strain which the necessarily prolonged spiritual struggle may entail, drugs have no value. The experience with drugs so far only goes to prove the fact that there are no shortcuts in spiritual life. The mass use of drugs by a very large section of world population may even prove detrimental to the evolutionary process of man.

Religion, Faith and Medicine

Search for Holistic Medicine

In modern times there is a trend towards holistic studies. There is a general disillusionment among intellectual circles all over the world with the Cartesian and Newtonian models of the world and their corresponding attitude towards life. The change in thinking began with the startling discoveries of modern sub-atomic physics. It became disillusionment as people began realizing the disastrous results of our ruthless exploitation of nature, which has now brought us near to the verge of ecological holocaust. Scientists, philosophers, and thinkers every where are searching for a new philosophy and a new way of life more wholesome and healthy. This probing and exploring has given rise to holistic sciences—holistic psychology, holistic medicine, biology and others. The "study of parts" as in the traditional classical sciences has proved inadequate for explaining integrated systems as a whole, and although compartmentalized studies are useful, they have to be complemented with another type of study which takes into consideration the integrated totality. In short, this is the attitude of the modern advocates of holistic sciences.

Modern western medicine too, is based upon the Cartesian subject-object dichotomy. Allopathic medicine studies the human being as a physical body made up of organs and cells. Thus to a doctor, the body appears something like a machine made up of cells, organs, joints, and muscles which functions due to electro-magnetic and chemical reactions. The great and astounding advances in medicine, especially in medical techonology, have taken place solely because of this mechanistic conceptualization of the human body. Unfortunately, however, the great successes and advances have strengthened the attachment of medical men to their present ways of thinking and doing things and their approaches towards their patients is becoming more and more technical rather than humane.

Man is not merely a body, or a conglomeration of cells, flesh, bones and blood. He also has a mind with complex emotions and thoughts. And he is a social being as well. Unless medical science takes into consideration all these aspects and treats the whole human being,—and not merely the human machine—it cannot be considered complete. In an attempt to obtain a holistic, complete system of medicine, in recent times there has been great interest and enquirey into various ancient systems of medicine like Ayurveda, the principles of Homoeopathy, Naturopathy, Chinese systems of medicine, etc.

Understandably, medical philosophers have shown interest even in primitive methods of healing, prevalent among the tribals and aboriginals. Faith healing and the role of religion in physical healing too have come under the searchlight of modern researches. We shall in this essay restrict ourselves to the relation and interaction between religion, faith and medicine.

Medicine and Religion are Poles Apart

There can be four ways in which this interaction between medicine and religion can be looked upon. According to the *first* approach, religion and medicine are thought of as two entirely different branches of human endeavour, having no relation with each other. Religion is based on faith, its goal is supernatural, other-worldly or entirely spiritual, and the means it employs to its ends are mostly psychological. Medicine on the other hand is a practical science based like any other empirical science on observable signs and symptoms, and laboratory data. Its goal is physical healing and the means employed are drugs, therapeutic procedures and nursing care. Thus the goal, the domain, and the means used are entirely different; the two have nothing in common between them. They are divergent human activities which have no meeting ground.

Often, religion in its crude, primitive, and ritualistic forms is considered a hindrance to the practice of rational and scientific medicine. Religion often breeds superstitions which prove detrimental to health. Diseases like smallpox and measles are thought by ignorant people to be caused by semi-divine beings who must be appeased and propitiated. Medical help is not sought and deaths and complications are the result. Such superstitious people are more often found in villages, though they are not altogether absent among the city dwellers.

The Common Goal

The *second view* is that religion and medicine may have different methodologies, but they have a common aim between them. Both are labouring to make humanity happier by eliminating suffering. True, religion emphasises the other-worldy aspect of existence and lays stress on happiness after death, but it also helps man to attain happiness in this life. It must be remembered that most people do not resort to religion for moksa or salvation, nor even for enjoying heavenly pleasures after death, but for the alleviation of worldly suffering (*arta*) and for the fulfilment of mundane desires (*artharthi*). The story of Dhruva as narrated in the Srimad Bhagavatam is an excellent illustration to the point. The child Dhruva, underwent the practice of severe austerities and prayed to Lord Vishnu not for moksha, but for obtaining the kingdom.

The story of Lord Buddha is another proof of the fact that both religion and medicine have a common aim in view. The young prince, Siddhartha, saw a sick man, an old person and a dead body. These scenes of physical suffering and death triggered a process of discrimination and enquiry into the ultimate cause of suffering and its soultion. Siddhartha finally became the Buddha and propagated a new religion. Interestingly, the triad: disease, old age, and death, which led to Gautama Buddha's enlightenment are the very foes against which medical science has been waging untiring war since time immemorial. The four basic aims of medicine are: the preservation of life (prevention or postponement of death); the alleviation of suffering; the prevention and cure of diseases; and the promotion of knowledge. Can religion ever be opposed to or disapprove of such noble aims? But, as already pointed out, the methodology and the philosophies behind these two branches are different. The Buddha preached the Eightfold Noble Path to extinguish all suffering, while medicine resots to physical means for the temporary alleviation of suffering and the cure of diseases. However, the Buddha, though the propounder of the path of righteous living, was never opposed to treatment of physical diseases. On the contrary, he personally set an example by nursing the sick.

Religion and Medicine are Complementary

The *third approach* can be to look upon religion and medicine as not only not contradictory, and not merely as serving the common goal, but as complementary to each other. A strong argument in favour of this view is the fact that medicine has originated out of religion. A study of the history of medicine shows that the earliest therapeutic procedures employed for physical ailments were mostly religious and ritualistic, such as propitiation of deities by religious rites, going on pilgrimages, chants and talismans, keeping vows, fasting on special days, making religious gifts, etc. This was known as *daiva-vyapasraya chikitsa,* cures depending on divine intercession. These practices were more prevalent at the time when medical science was not developed. But now with the accumulation of vast medical knowledge, the scope of their practice has narrowed and they are resorted to only in such incurable and problematic cases where medical science has not been able to contribute much. Many of these procedures have great psychological value for which they are often successfully employed.

Sickness as Strees

In recent times a phenomenal advancement in medical technology has made the modern medical man extremely powerful. He can detect smallest defects in structure and function of the human body with amazing accuracy. He can change a failing heart and can transplant a healthy kidney for a non-functioning one. He can work miracles with his tools of diagnosis and treatment and can infuse new life into patients who are almost dead. But when self-confidence becomes arrogance, he is apt to forget his limitations. Sri Ramakrishna, in his inimitable manner, describes the arrogance of the medical man: "God laughs... when the physician says to the mother weeping bitterly because of her child's desperate illness: 'Don't be afraid, mother, I shall cure your child.' The physician does not know that no one can save the child if God wills that he should die."[1] No one can better appreciate the truth of Sri Ramakrishna's statement than a conscientious physician.

In spite of all the technological advancements in the medical sciences, man has not been able to conquer disease, old age and death. If some fatal diesease has been brought under control, newer ones have cropped up. Uncertainty regarding the outcome of disease processes looms large in many cases, and unequal distribution of available medical facilities continue to maintain the scarcity situation in an unjust society. With all the wondrous modern equipment medical man continues to be uncertain, only marginally powerful, and certainly incapable of providing help to all. Thus the three inevitable situations, viz, uncertainty,

---

1. 'M', *The Gospel of Sri Ramakrishna* (Madras: Sri Ramakrishna Math, Mylapore, 1986) p. 324.

helplessness and scarcity, for which religion too tries to seek an answer, continue to exist in the field of medicine as well.

Every disease is a stress situation and every surgical operation an uncertainty for the patient and his relatives. Hence those who are less fortunate and less equipped physically, monetarily and psychologically naturally resort to some form of religion and faith for consolation and support. Even in a technologically advanced society, human ventures, however carefully planned and expertly executed, are liable to end in disapointment or failure. Emotional involvement in such situations leads to deep psychological stress and man is led to breaking points. Religion comes to help at such points by supplying a supra-empirical view of a larger total reality. The theory of *Karma*, the concept of life after death, the faith in divine dispensations, the will of God, and so on, are the solutions which religion offers to sustain the patients as well as to provide a holistic dimension. During such stress situations a doctor can invite a priest or a religious man to help the patient and his relatives to bear the crisis. Unlike a majority of their colleagues, some doctors themselves resort to prayer and appreciate its value for themselves and their patients.

Faith, a Great Healer

It is recorded that Jesus Christ used to cure blindness, drive away ghosts, and even raise the dead by his mere touch or command. But there is one striking incident in his life, which highlights the power of faith as a healing factor. Once while Jesus was passing through a road, a great crowd followed and thronged about him. A woman who was suffering from 'flow of blood' for twelve years touched his garment syaing to herself that if she touched even his garment she would be cured. Immediately the bleeding stopped. Jesus realized that power had gone forth from him and turning around asked who had touched him, although a great crowd was pressing around him. When the lady who had touched him told him the truth, Jesus told her, "Daughter, your faith has made you well; go in peace and be healed of your disease."[1]

2. *The New Testament;* The Gospel according to St. Mark, 5. 25-34.

A funny story is narrated of a villager who visited a doctor for his ailments. He was examined and was given a prescription written on a piece of paper. A few months later, fully cured and healthy, he came back to pay his respects to the doctor. Unable to recognize the patient by his looks, the doctor wanted to remember him with the help of his written prescription. When asked for it, the patient, now cured, pointed to the amulet on his arm. The patient was cured by the paper worn on the arm as an amulet!

These are two extreme examples of healing produced by the power of faith. They may or may not be true, but they do highlight the value of faith in the physician as a healing factor. More authentic records of faith healing are found in the life of the Holy Mother, Sri Sarada Devi. She had firm faith that the earth within the precincts of Godddess Simhavahini Devi's temple at Jayrambati could cure ailments if applied to the affected part. Cases of snake bite are on record which got cured by the application of the earth on the bitten part.

Psychosomatic Diseases

Just as physical suffering leads to anxiety and mental stress, so also worry, anxiety and psychological tensions affect the body and cause diseases. These are called psychosomatic diseases. Peptic ulcer, asthma, diabetes, hypertension, neurodermatosis and others are sometimes caused and sustained by worry, anxiety, fear, frustration, jealousy, etc. The fast pace of modern life with its rigid fixation with the clock is causing tremendous stress, leading to hypertension and heart diseases. Hostile emotional reactions not only consume lot of psychic energy, but they can also precipitate serious problems, like the perforation of a peptic ulcer. A greedy person is more liable to develop diabetes than a contented one. An over-ambitious person is more prone to hypertension, and an emotionally high strung one runs greater risk of having an attack of stroke.

These observations have led to rapid growth and popularity of psychiatry and psychotherapy. But more than palliative and superficial psychiatric help, what most patients with psychosomatic disease need is a healthy way of living and a right attitude towards life, which religion can provide. Religion teaches how not to become a prey to greed and anger and thus helps one to avoid psychosomatic problems. This is the reason why Yoga is becoming extremely popular, not only as a treatment for diseases like diabetes, asthma and hypertension, but also as a way to a healthy tension-free life.

Medical Ecology and Shamanism

Shamanism is another offshoot of primitive religion which is practised for the treatment of physical ailments. A shaman or witch-doctor claims to have contact with gods and is supposed to suggest divine remedies. In recent years some Western anthropologists have tried to study shamanism as prevalent among tribal people. Belgian anthropologist Professor R. Pinxten, with his many years of experience with Navajo Indians, feels that shamanistic medicine is more holistic than Western medical science. The Western view regards an illness as a local and isolated phenomenon.

The patient is seldom regarded 'wholistically' in the socio-ethnic context. Conversely, the shamanistic view is that all elements must be in harmony. Sickness is the result of a disturbance in the relationships between people and other living beings, between people and their ancestors, etc. Each individual has a place in, and is a part of, the social order. The shamanist healer is the person who finds out where that order had been disrupted and indicates how that harmony can be restored (through ceremonies, for example). Dr. Cl. Farrer, an American anthropologist working among the Mescaler Apache Indians, has come to a similar conclusion: "In contrast to the Western mode of thought, Apache know that suffering, illness, pain and grief occur when the inherent balance of life is upset. Only by reasserting properness and reestablishing the ethnic relationships among people and the other aspects of the creation can rupture causing illness, suffering, pain and grief be mended."[1]

---

1. "Ethical Reflections on Health and Illness," *Sion Conference 1990-91; The Netherlands. First written symposium*. Introduction, *p. iv.*

A large number of ecological factors affect human health. The effect of climatic changes on the body is well recognized. Astrology claims that the course of diseases can be influenced by stars and planets. Based on this concept a number of ritualistic procedures and ceremonies have been evolved to counteract the bad effects of these astrological factors. Though not directly a part of religion, these ceremonies are akin to religious ritualistic practices. This astrological view is not unscientific and can be combined, if necessary, with other medical means and procedures. Sri Ramakrishna indicated by his obervances and by his example that all these have an element of truth in them.

Religion the Best Medicine

The *fourth and final approach* can be not to consider religion and medicine as separate. According to this view, religion is the best medicine and medical science is the best religion in practice. Since religion tries to remove suffering by going to its very root, it is considered the best medicine. The cycle of repeated births and deaths is spoken of in religious parlance as *bhava-roga*, an afflicition or disease, and God is called the Physician—*bhava-roga-Vaidya, Vaidya-Narayano-Harih*. Lord Buddha is similarly referred to as *Mahabhisaka*, physician par-excellence, also *Sallakatta*, surgeon.

Again, this view looks at evil propensities not merely as the cause of physical ailments but as diseases themselves. According to Tulsidas, the author of the great epic, *Ramacharit Manas:*

Delusion is the root of all ailments (of the soul) and from this again spring many pains. The flatulence of lust, the phlegm of insatiable greed, and the bile of passion constantly inflame the breast, and when these three combine, there results a miserable paralysis of the whole system. Who can tell the names of all the diseases represented by the various obstinate sensual cravings? Such are the leprosy of selfishness, the itch of envy, the reheumatic throbs of joy and sorrow, the consumption that burns at the sight of another's prosperity, the horrible open sore of malignant spirit, the excruciating gout of egoism, the sciatica of heresy, hypocrisy, vanity, pride, and so on.[1]

A similar description of the symptoms of the afflicted soul is found in a Bengali song Sri Ramakrishna used to sing:

What a delirious fever is this that
    I suffer from!
O Mother, Thy grace is my only cure.
False pride is the fever that rocks my
    wasted form;
"I" and "mine" are my cry. Oh, what a
    wicked delusion!
My quenchless thirst for wealth and
    friends is never-ceasing:
How, then, shall I sustain my life?
Talk about things unreal, this is my
    wretched delirium,
And I indulge in it always, O Giver of
    all good fortune!
My eyes in seeming sleep are closed,
    my stomach is filled
With the vile worms of cruelty.

------

1. *The Ramayana of Tulsidas,* Tr. E.S. Growse, 6th Edition, Ramanarayanlal, Allahabad, p. 671.

Alas! I wander about absorbed in
        unmeaning deeds;
Even for Thy holy name I have no taste,
        O Mother!
I doubt that I shall ever be cured of this
        malady.[1]

What are the remedies suggested?

Pious religious observances, penance, meditation, sacrifice, prayer, and almsgiving are so many different remedies. By the grace of Rama every disease is extirpated if the treatment is conducted in the following manner: with the holy teacher for physician, faith for a prescription, contempt of the world for regimen, devotion to Hari for life giving drug, and a soul full of faith for the vehicle in which it is administered...[2]

That none can be truly healthy without a healthy mind was the opinion of Plato in ancient times. "No attempt should be made to cure the body without the soul," he said, "and if the head and body aught

---

1. *The Gospel of Sri Ramakrishna*, pp. 203-04
2. *The Ramayana*, p. 672.

to be healthy, you must begin by curing the mind."[1] Thus, religion can indeed by looked upon as the best medicine. While an average physician cannot possibly rise to the spiritual heights of a Buddha or a Christ, he can certainly become a better physician by imbibing spiritual values and being himself a religious man. "Blessed is he who carries within himself a God, an ideal of beauty... for therein lie springs of great thoughts and great action,"[2] said Louis Pasteur the great scientist.

A physician is in an excellent position to act as a spiritual healer of his patient. By his position as a physician, he acquires certain privileges which are denied to others. He can come in close psychological, spiritual and confessional relationship with the patient. A patient seeks an unshakable ally in whom he can unburden the deep and complex problems of his life. He needs someone who can listen to him patiently and to whom he can disclose his secret

1. Udupa and Gurumohan Singh, *"Religion & Medicine"*, Institute of Medicical Sciences, BHU, Varanasi, 1974, p. 9.

2. *Ibid.*

worries and feelings of guilt, someone who can understand problems and sympathise without moralizing or accusing. A deeply religious doctor can do this job much better.

Medicine—The Best Practical Religion

Finally, let us see how the practice of medicine can become one of the best forms of practical religion. According to Swami Vivekananda, a human being is the best and highest temple of God. To consider the sick and suffering as veritable embodiments of God, and to serve them in the spirit of consecration is the first condition for transforming medical practice into a religious act.

The commonest form of worship prevalent among most religions is the ritualistic worship of a symbol of God such as an image, a picture, or a pitcher, or other forms. First of all, ritualistically, life is infused into the lifeless symbol. This is followed by purification of the articles of worship. After such preliminaries, the worshipper offers five, ten or sixteen items to the deity with the help of ritual acts and the chanting of verbal formulae or *mantras*. Such deeply sacred acts can be performed while serving a human being, looking upon him as an embodiment of divinity. Instead of flowers and incense, tablets and mixtures are administered; instead of water for bathing an image, a patient is sponged or bathed with medicated lotion. Application of ointments or dressing a wound may be compared to offering sandalpaste to the Deity. An amiable manner and reassuring words of hope to the patient are like *mantras* in the worship of God.

While the general outline of the process of worship is the same, the items offered and the mantras chanted vary from diety to deity. The mantras and items employed in the worship of Kali are not those used in the worship of Siva. Similarly, there are differences in the form of medical service given to patients suffering from typhoid, meningitis or intestinal obstruction. Indeed, a surgical operation can be compared to an elaborate Durga Puja. The operation theatre is the *Puja mandapam*, worship hall; the chief surgeon is the chief priest conducting the solemn ceremony of the operation ritual with the help of his team of assistants. The elaborate preparations, the perfect solemnity and careful method and procedure—all are comparable to those of a Durga Puja.

Service to a suffering human being as God is even superior to a ritualistic worship. While one has to imagine or ritualistically infuse life into a stone image, nothing of the sort is required in serving a man as God, for he is already alive. There is a far greater manifestation of divinity in a living human being. Secondly, serving God in man helps both the server and the served, while the traditional worship helps only the worshipper. Finally, serving a human being as God requires greater intellectual, moral and spiritual training than is required for ritual-worship.

But seeing or feling the presence of God in a miserable, poor, ignorant, suffering patient is not easy. A physician is apt to see in his patient only man or woman, rich or poor, saint or sinner, or a fellow being of high or low caste. The human God may grunt or complain, and unlike the mute ever-smiling stone image, may weep, shout or at times become irritable or violent.

On such occasions one is apt to wonder whether one is serving God or devil.

The service of a living God, therefore, demands greather patience, forbearance and persevernace. Repeatedly the physician will have to remind himself that the being in front of him is not a man or a woman, but God Himself. He will have to overcome his reactions of disinterestedness, irritation, annoyance and replulsion—disinterestedness, because a patient may not present any fascinating clinical problem; irritation at the patient's verbosity, lack of consistency and clarity in giving the history of his condition; annoyance, because the patient does not follow his instructions or because the disease does not respond to treatment as expected, and repulsion, because of the patient's lack of cleanliness, self-control, or absense of a sense of intelligent cooperation.

The service of God in man is therefore a training in itself, a process of character building, and a spiritual practice of the highest order. It demands an intelligent combination of technical skill, human understanding and spiritual and religious values. All those persons who engage in serving the sick, the diseased, or otherwise needy, are indeed most blessed and fortunate.

We may best summarise the purport of the inserparable relation between the practice of religion and the practice of medicine in the words of Sister Nivedita as she explained the practical philosophy of Vedanta in the light of Sri Ramakrishna's and Vivekananda's teachings: "No distinction, henceforth," she said, "between sacred and secular. To labour is to pray. To conquer is to renounce. Life is itself religion. To have and to hold is as stern a trust as to quit and to avoid..."[1] And as Vivekananda himself said, "...the workshop, the study, the farmyard, and the field are as true and fit scenes for the meeting of God with man as the cell of the monk or the door of the temple. To him there is no difference between service of man and worship of God, between manliness and faith, between true righteousness and spirituality."[2] ✤

---

1. *The Complete Works of Swami Vivekananda* (Calcutta: Advaita Ashrama, 1984) "*Introduction*", by Sister Nivedita, p. xv.

2. *Ibid.*, pp. xv-xvi.

Turning Towards
Swami Vivekananda
for Health - I

"My ideal can indeed be put into a few words and that is to preach unto mankind their divinity and how to make it manifest in every movement of life,"[1] Swami Vivekananda worte to Sister Nivedita. For he knew that the knowledge of one's divinity would make a teacher a better teacher, a student a better student; indeed, it would make an individual a better individual in every way. It is certain that Swamiji's message would make a doctor a better doctor, and even a patient, a better, more calm and cooperative patient. But that is not all. Swamiji has message for not only the doctor, the patient and the nurse, but for the medical world as a whole.

---

1. *The Complete Works of Swami Vivekananda* (Calcutta : Advaita Ashrama, 1989) Vol. 7, page 501.

We are passing through an age of rapidly changing concepts in every branch of knowledge. In the sphere of applied sciences there is constant search for appropriate or alternative technology. Like so many institutions of contemporary society, modern medicine too has come under the fire of criticism and the goal and the practice of medicine today are being questioned. At such a turning point it will be wise to pause and look towards Swami Vivekananda for guidance. However, before we study the implications of Swamiji's message for the medical science, let us first have a clear idea of what health and medicine are, and what the situation at present is.

Health, a Neglected Entity

Health had always remained one of the most neglected aspects of life. On the individual level it is subordinated to other so-called more important needs like wealth, power, prestige, knowledge, security, etc. Health is often taken for granted and one becomes conscious of its value only when it is lost. One of the reasons for its neglect is that the human system has a number of adaptive mechanisms which come into play during periods of stress and prevent the body from breakdown.

At the international level health was overlooked—"forgotten"—when the covenant of the League of Nations was drafted after the first world war. World Health Organization (WHO) was founded in 1945[1] while the charter of the UNO was being drafted. During the past few decades there has been a re-awakening of interest in health and it has been recognized as a fundamental human right and a worldwide social goal, which is called "Health for All". At the national level too, health remained neglected. Only 2% of the national outlay for the seventh 5-year-plan was alloted for health.[2] The total budget for health is less than one percent of India's gross national product—a level that compares unfavourably with Zambia, Jordan or Tunisia, Chile or Mexico, Kenya or Ethiopia—leave alone China or Brazil.[3]

---

1. Park, J.E. & Park, K., *Textbook of Preventive and Social Medicine,* 12th edition. (Jabalpur, M/S Banarasidas Bhanot, 1989) page 11.

2. *Ibid.,* page 15.

3. Bidwai, P., "Public Hospitals Turning Into Illness Factories," *The Times of India,* August 3, 1992, page 1.

What is Health?

Like all abstract terms, "health" is difficult to define. Neither the determinants of health are clear, nor is there a single yardstick for measuring it. Besides, there are many levels of health and sickness between positive health and death, and many people live at the level of unrecognized sickness or mild sickness, which does not force them to become inactive :

Positive health
Better health
Freedom from Sickness

Unrecognized sickness
Mild sickness
Severe sickness

Death
(*Health-Sickness Spectrum*)[1]

The Sanskrit word for health is *swasthya*, which means etymologically, to be established in one's natural state. Traditionally, health is defined as absence

1. Park and Park, page 15.

of disease, and disease as deviation from biological norm. According to this bio-medical concept, the body is looked upon as a machine and disease means its breakdown. The doctor's task is to repair this biological machine. This working model is accepted by most practising doctors. However this concept of physical health is inadequate to explain and solve some major problems of health: e.g., malnutrition, accidents, drug-abuse, mental illness, etc. which point at social and psychological dimensions.

Ecology of health is the study of the relation between variations in man's environment and his state of health, and from this standpoint health is defined as a state of dynamic equilibrium between man and his environment. When this balance between the virulence of the causative agent and the resistance of the human host is disturbed in favour of the former, disease occurs. It has been recognized that the control of diseases by environmental manipulation is much cheaper, safer, effective and rational, than the treatment of individual cases. Thus, there are social, cultural, and psychological factors in relation to health. It is not possible to raise the level of people's health without changing their social environment, living habits, and culturally acquired unhealthy practices. This concept has given rise to a very important branch called "social medicine".

The above concepts are embodied in the WHO definition of health: "Health is a state of complete physical, mental and social well-being and not merely an absence of disease or infirmity."[1] This definition, however, considers health a state, while health is more a process of continuous adjustment to the changing demands of living. In this context health is defined as "a state of relative equilibrium of body form and function, which results from its successful dynamic adjustment to forces tending to disturb it."[2] Positive health implies "the perfect functioning of the body and mind in a given social milieu." It is the ideal, the goal, towards which people should strive.

---

1. *Ibid.*, page 12.
2. *Ibid.*, page 12.

In recent years a newer, holistic concept of health has been evolved. This concept recognizes the strength of social, economic, environmental, and even political influences on health. Health is now recognized as a multidimensional and an inter-sectorial process. It is now an intergral part of development and is the essence of productive life. It involves individual, group, state, and international responsibility. That health is a worldwide social goal had been highlighted by the launching of the WHO movement, called "*Health for All by the Year 2000*". The world assembly referred to it as "the attainment by all the people of the world to a level of health that will permit them to lead a socially and economically productive life."[1]

There is difference between "Health care service for all" and "Health for all". Health services can be available to all but neither be relevant to the needs of all, nor used by all. Hence one of the important themes of the "Health for all" programme

1. WHO (1978), *Health for All,* Sr. No. 1. quoted by Park & Park, page 9.

was, "Universal coverage with primary health care, that is relevant, effective, acceptable and affordable in terms of the needs, cultural interests and resources of each community." "Health for all" had posed new challenges before the medical world as well as the governments of various countries. Now even a conscientious citizen cannot remain content with taking care of his own health and observing his own rules of health and hygiene, nor can a doctor restrict his sphere of activity to his patients only. He may act locally but must at least think globally.

Changing Concepts of Medicine

Like the concepts of health, medicine too had been evolving and changing. Conceived in sympathy and born out of necessity, medicine is as old as man himself. It began as religion and art and gradually evolved into a science. In prehistoric times (circa 5000 B.C.) medicine was intermingled with religion, superstition, magic and witchcraft.

Modern medicine got a boost during the Renaissance (14th-16th centuries A.D.)

Progress since then had been rapid with discoveries of circulation (by Harvey in 1628), the microscope (1670), vaccination against smallpox (1796), etc. By the close of the 19th century the dicotomy of medicine into two major branches, namely curative and preventive medicine (or public health), was evident.

Curative Medicine

The aim of curative medicine is the elimination of disease from an individual patient rather than from the community. Over the years curative medicine has advanced phenomenally and has accumulated vast scientific knowledge, technical skills, medicaments and highly sophisticated instruments and apparatuses for diagnosis and treatment.

During the last few decades there has been a tremendous growth in specializations. Some specializations are based on skills, such as surgery, medicine, radiology, anaesthesiology; some are based on the part of body, e.g., ENT, ophthalmology, etc. Other specialities are based on particular age or sex: e.g., paediatrics, geriatrics, obstetrics, etc. Again there are sub-specialities within each speciality, for example, neonatology (dealing with disease of the new-born), paediatric-surgery, paediatric neurology—all in paediatrics. One wonders if such micro or super-specialization is really needed. Specialization has raised the standard of medical care but it has escalated the cost of medical care tremendously, placing it beyond the means of an average citizen.

Preventive Medicine

As the name indicates, the primary objective of preventive medicine is prevention of diseases and promotion of health. Hence it applies mainly to healthy people. Early advances in preventive medicine were in the field of bacterial vaccines and sera which led to the conquest of a number of diseases. The eradication of smallpox was its greatest achievement. Discoveries in nutrition helped in the prevention of diseases like nutritional blindness and iodine deficiency goitre. The discovery of synthetic insecticides like DDT, melathion, etc. has brought about a fundamental change in the strategy of combating vector-borne diseases, like plague, malaria, leishmaniasis, chemoprophylaxis (prevention by use of chemical agents or drugs), and mass drug treatment are other tools for control of infectious diseases.

In modern times preventive medicine is faced with another kind of problem i.e., population explosion which has stimulated research in human fertility, contraceptive technology and genetics. Also the so-called life-style diseases like diabetes, high blood pressure, heart diseases, and accidents, AIDS, etc. have now come under the purview of preventive medicine. Indeed, as medical science advances it will become more and more preventive medical practice, of which three levels are recognized. Primary prevention intends to prevent disease among healthy people; secondary is directed towards those in whom disease is already developed, and tertiary aims at restricting the chronic disability consequent upon disease.

Social Medicine

With the advancement of medicine the cost of medical care increased and two types of medicare came into existence: one for the rich and the other for the poor. The gap was, and is, bridged to a small extent by charitable and voluntary agencies providing free medical care to the poor. In Germany 'Socialization of medicine' was tried by compulsory sickness insurance in 1883, followed by England and France. However Russia was the first to socialize medicine completely and to give to its citizens constitutional rights to all health services. Since then this has been tried in many countries including India (ESIS). Social medicine considers medicine as a social science and covers almost every subject in the field of health and welfare, medical needs and medical care of society.

Family Mdicine

This is the branch of medicine which is neither disease-oriented nor organ-oriented, but which is oriented to the health care of a family as a unit—from first contact to the ongoing care of chronic problems and from prevention to rehabilitation. Specialization in medicine has caused fragmentation of the medical care delivery and produced cleavage in the doctor-patient relationship. Hence now a great need is felt for a general practitioner who could provide such a family oriented medical care.

Palliative and Placebo Medicine

This is not a scientific branch of medicine but the name given to the practice which aims only at relieving symptoms without curing the disease. Not all patients who approach a doctor suffer from specific diseases. According to one estimate 40% of all patients seeking medical help from dispensaries, outpatient departments and health centres, have no obvious organic disorder.[1] These patients are prescribed non-specific drugs for relief of their symptoms only.

Placebo effect is a well known phenomenon in the medical circles. It is observed that dummy pills when used as control while trying a new drug give a positive response

1. King, M.H. "Medicine in An Unjust World" in *The Oxford Textbook of Medicine* (London : ELBS, Oxford University Press, 1985) pp. 3-5

in a third of cases.[1] Making use of this fact, doctors often use so-called tonics and other drugs without having much medicinal value, simply to satisfy or to cheer up the patients. And for various reasons, mostly psychological, such drugs do prove effective in alleviating symptoms. Patients do not bother about the pharmaceutical properties of drugs, or how they act. They want relief and this need is exploited by the drug companies and the doctors.

Commercial Medicine

This again is not a subsection of medicine, but a phrase coined to express business trends in a profession which must fulfil a benign and not a selfish purpose, which must be protective and not exploitative and which cannot have any analogy with business. Yet it is unfortunate that medical world is taking the shape of a big industry and profit earning business. Medical research involves huge expenses

---

1. Vyas, B.K., & Nene, D.V., *Towards Holistic Health* (Baroda : Academy of Holistic Health, 1990) page 120.

and when a new drug or a diagnostic procedure or instrument—a product of such research—is launched in the market, the manufacturers are naturally anxious to create a good market for it. Hence the drug etc. is launched with great publicity and advertising as the best product ever produced. The benefits are over-emphasized and the limitations not even mentioned. The manufacturing firms are motivated purely by profit and all possible methods are used to induce the doctors to prescribe the drug. The whole network involves monetary interests of influencial and powerful groups. "The present day structure of medicare acts like a huge industrial empire. The lucrative gains are such as to attract investors in a big way to commercially exploit the market. Even in the sale of a single drug, many master-minds get motivated through machiavellian methods."[1]

Although everyone is a consumer of health services, consumerism has produced a cleavage in the doctor-patient relationship where trust and sympathy were once

---

1. *Ibid.*, page 122.

fundamental. Now-a-days this relationship has degraded into a commercial transaction where both parties are suspicious of the other's intentions. This leads not only to loss of precious human dimensions but also to substandard care. Endless investigations are ordered and a long list of drugs prescribed—which might otherwise be superfluous—simply to protect the doctor or to satisfy the patient or worse still, to obtain the commission offered by a laboratory or pharmaceutical firm. The present day open market economy has made the situation worse. Even otherwise modern medical care has become extremely expensive and a cause for grave concern, even in an affluent country like the U.S.A. where falling sick is one of the major causes of bankruptcy.[1]

Success and Failure of Medicine

It cannot be denied that modern medicine has made spectacular advances. It has moved from organism to organ, from organ to cell, from cell to the molecular properties. Marvellous discoveries of nucleic acid

---

1. "Medicine in An Unjust World", pp. 3-6.

and genetic code have paved the way to genetic counselling, genetic engineering, prenatal diagnosis of sex, etc. Organ transplantation, artificial heart and kidneys, psycho-surgery, etc. are amazing marvels of modern medicine.

However, there is a dark side too. Despite spectatcular advancements and massive expenditure, death rates and life-expectancy even in developed countries have remained unchanged. Whatever improvement in longevity has occurred, it has been due to improved sanitation and good supply and not due to high technology. Increasing medical costs have not led to increased benefits, and some believe that the limit of health impact of modern medical care and research have been reached.

The threat posed by major diseases like malaria, amaebiasis, filaria, leprosy have not lessened, or have even increased. Infant and child mortality rates in developing countries continue to remain high. There is no equality in distribution of health services, resulting in limited access to health care for a large segment of the population. 80% of health expenditure is spent on 20%

of urban population and 20% for the 80% rural population.[1] Having an elitistic orientation and under the pressure of high technology, medical care systems are going away from health promotion for many towards expensive treatment for the few. Unfortunately in developing countries there is a tendency to follow the western model of medical education and favour the high cost, low-coverage, elite oriented health service. Even the efficacy of modern medicine is fundamentally questioned and some critics have described modern medicine as a threat to health. Such a state is labelled as "Failure of success".[2]

Alternative Systems of Medicine

This failure of medicine to promote health for all has stimulated search for other systems of medicine. Most societies and cultures have their own medical systems and beliefs. Apart from folk medicine and folk healing, Indian, Chinese, and Persian medicines having written traditions are

---

1. *Ibid.*, page 3.
2. Park & Park, page 8.

based on empirical knowledge and are practised by professional elite. Then there is the so-called popular medicine, consisting of beliefs and practices within a family and a community which are passed by word of mouth and mostly the prerogative of the women folk.[1]

So far modern medicine had claimed to be the only true medicine and alternatives were labelled as quackery. This stance is changing. Interest in alternatives is growing in the West. Ayurveda is being studied deeply. Homeopathy is already being widely practised and at times by doctors trained in allopathic medicine. Psychotherapy is already well established, while hypnotism is being increasingly practised with dramatic results. Parallel to an emerging concept of holistic health, there is a trend towards holistic medicine, although the concept is not yet clear.

For a medicine to be holistic, it must not only be universally applicable but must also cover all aspects of health—physical,

---

1. Capra, Fritjof, *The Turning Point* (New York: Flamingo, 1989) page 121.

mental, social and spiritual. Some Indian doctors have attempted to evolve a concept of holistic medicine on the basis of the Vedantic concept of the five *Koshas*.[1]

The Hospitals

Since hospitals play very important role in the health care system, it will be pertinent here to study their evolution and functions. A hospital is not a static organization. It is subject to change in structure and function according to the change in the needs of the community. A century ago a hospital was something like a place of refuge for the sick and the homeless. It was a charitable institution where old people approaching death got shelter. The appeal written by Swami Vivekananda for the Ramakrishna Mission Home of Service, Varanasi, in February 1902 relates to this very function of a hospital.[2]

In contrast, the hospitals today are concerned with active medical treatment

---

1. Vyas & Nene, page 1.
2. Swami Vivekananda, *The Complete Works*, Vol. 5, page 436.

utilizing all the latest knowledge of medical science and technology. Earlier they were occupied by the old and the poor. Now they are occupied by all classes of people, as is evident from the free-beds, paying-beds, semi-private and private rooms. Earlier a single doctor could provide single handed all the skills needed for treatment. Now there is an increasing demand for specialists in each department.

Teaching, both medical and nursing, and research are the other functions of a modern hospital. Rural and district hospitals, however, concentrate on patient care. It is said that each hospital has a personality of its own—a tempo of work and an emotional atmosphere, its traditions and its community of staff and patients. All these together create specific atmospheres of different hospitals. Some have a good name and some have a bad one.

The hospital system also is not without fault and of late, has come under the fire of criticism. The hospital medical practice has progressively become depersonalized if not dehumanized. Hospitals have grown into professional institutions emphasizing technology and scientific competence rather than contact with patients as human beings. They exist in splendid isolation from the broader health problems of the community, acquiring the euphemism "ivory tower of disease". The treatment is expensive and the hospitals absorb vast proportion of the health budget–50% to 80%.[1] Some 30% to 50% of present hospitalization is unnecessary medically, but alternative services that could be therapeutically effective and economical are disappearing.

In 1957 an expert committee of WHO emphasized that the hospital cannot work in isolation. It must be a part of a system that provides complete health care to the population. Subsequent years witnessed efforts of WHO, UNICEF and non-government agencies to involve hospitals in providing basic and referral services. The establishment of primary health centres was a step towards integration of curative and preventive medicine.

Dr. Rene Sand has said that "the right patient should receive the right care at the

---

1. Park & Park, page 41.

right time in the right place and at the right cost."[1] The medicare system with the hospital at the centre must be such a flexible system capable of adapting itself to the total health care needs of the community.

This overview of health, concepts of medicine and the hospitals is meant not only for information but to prepare a ground for the better understanding of the implications of Swami Vivekananda's message for the medical world. Scholars and thinkers in every field of knowledge have realized that the deep significance of the teachings of Swami Vivekananda can be grasped only after having a thorough theoretical knowledge and practical experience of that subject. Hence this long introductory note.

---

1. Rene Sand. *The Advance to Social Medicine* (London : Staples Press, 1952) quoted by Park & Park, page 41.

Turning Towards Swami Vivekananda for Health - II

$\mathcal{W}$e have seen in the foregoing review that through ages the concepts of health and medicine had been evolving and changing. Medicine evolved from being curative to being preventive, from preventive to social, and from social to community oriented. Today its principal value is "health" and its goal is "health for all". In 1977 it was decided in the Health Assembly of WHO to launch the "Health for All" movement. This was reaffirmed at Alma Ata in 1978 and endorsed by the UNO General Assembly in 1981. The Alma Ata Conference observed that "the gross inequality in the health status of people, particularly between developed and developing countries as well as within countries is politically, socially and economically unacceptable."[1]

---

1. Park,J.E. and Park,K., *Text Book of Preventive and Social Medicine*, 12th ed., (Jabalpur: M/S. Banarasidas Bhanot, 1989), page 9.

Swami Vivekananda was deeply aware of the inequality and injustice prevailing in society, and was intensely sensitive to the miseries of the unprivileged masses. Almost three quarters of a century before the Alma Ata declaration, he had suggested some remedies which are even more relevant today. Let us therefore turn towards him for guidance for the fulfillment of the goal of "Health for all." It must be remembered that Swamiji based all his teachings on the Vedantic truth of the divinity of man and the unity of existence.

Swamiji's Message for the Sick

Swami Vivekananda has a message for the ailing person. He believed that Vedantic truths can drive away disease. He wrote to his ailing brother disciple: "Even the poison of a snake is powerless if you can firmly deny it."[1] And again: "Why are Baburam and Yogen suffering so much? It is owing to their negative, their self abasing spirit. Tell them to brush aside their

---

1. *The Complete Works of Swami Vivekananda*, (Calcutta: Advaita Ashrama, 1978), Vol.VI, page 275.

illness by mental strength, and in an hour illness will disappear. I the Atman smitten with disease! Off with it! Tell them to meditate for an hour at a stretch, 'I am the Atman, how can I be affected by disease!' —and everything will vanish. Think all of you that you are the infinite powerful Atman and see what strength comes out.... I *am*, God *is*, everything is in me. I *will* manifest health, purity, knowledge, whatever I want.... Who says you are ill—what is disease to you? Brush it aside!... Repeat to yourself that such and such are Atman, that they are infinite, and how can they have any disease? Repeat this an hour or so on a few successive days and all disease and trouble will vanish into naught."[1] "Whenever any one of you is sick, let him himself or anyone of you visualise him in your mind, and mentally say and strongly imagine that he is all right. That will cure him quickly. You can do it even without his knowledge, and even with thousands of miles between you."[2]

---

1. *Ibid.*, pp.276-77.
2. *Ibid.*, Vol.V, 1985, page 33.

Message for the Medical Personnel

For doctors and those who are engaged in the service of the sick, Swamiji's message is even more pertinent and explicit. He urges them to serve the patients as the veritable embodiments of God. "Serving man as God" is the *Yuga-dharma*, the religion for the present age. This attitude turns a secular act into a consecrated one and service of men into the best form of worship of the divine. In this worship of the patient-God, the physician or the surgeon is the chief priest, the nurse, the compounder, the assistants, the anaesthetists and others are his helpers; and the objects of worship (*upacaara* or *upakarana*) are the tablets, injections, ointments, infusions, etc. A surgical operation in its elaborate preparation, solemnity, and methodical procedure can be fairly compared to an elaborate Durga Puja.

But the mere attitude of mind considering the patient as God is not enough. For a true servant of the people, Swamiji lays down a few important conditions. For all would-be reformers, patriots and social servants, Swamiji says: "Three things are necessary for great achievements. First feel from the heart. Do you feel that the millions of descendants of gods and of sages have become next-door neighbours to brutes... that is the first step."[1] The second condition is to find out a way, a practical solution to the problem before us. And the third condition is the steadfastness, the will, the determination to pursue the path one has chosen, against all difficulties and hindrances. In other words none can truly and effectively serve the sick unless he has a feeling heart and real love and sympathy, nor until he has learnt the necessary skills to serve, irrespective of any return in the form of money, name, or fame, or recognition, and until he can face all difficulties like financial stringency, social unfairness or blame, or withdrawal of cooperation. The relevance of the above conditions laid down by Swamiji for an ideal medical worker can be immediately appreciated if we look at the prevailing medical scene in India. Due to lack of feeling this noble method of service, the medical profession,

---

1. *Ibid.*, Vol.III, 1984, page 225.

is getting converted into a trade and an ugly method of exploitation; due to lack of proper knowledge it is being reduced to quackery, and without the necessary determination to pursue, it is leading to negligence and incomplete treatment.

Incidentally, it may be mentioned that with all his love for India and revolutionary sociological ideas about the uplift of the masses, Swamiji did not try for national independence soon after his return from the West. Asked why he was not more outspoken for India's freedom from the British rule, Swamiji said that India lacked men who could safeguard the freedom if obtained. Hence, he instead established the Belur Math and opened centres for man-making and character building. This need for character is also evident in the field of medicine. The unethical practices prevailing at present in India in the medical field underscore Swami Vivekananda's message of the need for man-making and character-building. Suffice it to say that the doctors and the paramedical personnel must first of all be men endowed with something of Buddha's heart and Sankara's intellect with a gigantic will capable of surmounting all difficulties.

Food, Water and Sanitation

Let us now turn to the wider issues concerning health. Swami Vivekananda may not have spoken directly about health and medicine, but he has given enough hints by which the health of the masses can be improved, diseases can be prevented and mortality can be reduced. Swamiji believed in total eradication of disease. "My method of treatment is to take out by the roots the very causes of the disease and not to keep them merely suppressed."[1] This was told in the context of social reform, and Swamiji also pointed out the root causes of all ills. They were, in short, poverty and ignorance.[2] The Indian masses had very little to eat and were ignorant about the basic laws of health. "The poor die of starvation because they can get nothing to eat, and the rich die of starvation because what they take is not food."[3] Swamiji gave an illustration about

1. *Ibid.*, Vol.V, page 334.
2. *Ibid.*, Vol.VI, page 225.
3. *Ibid.*, Vol.V, page 486-87.

the ignorance of the Indians about food: "Suppose the head of the firm gets displeased with someone and decreases his pay; or out of three or four bread winning sons in a family, one suddenly dies, what do they do? Why, they at once curtail the quantity of milk for the children, or live on one meal a day having a little puffed rice or so at night!" When asked what else can be done, Swamiji replied, "Why, can't they exert themselves and earn more to keep up their standard of food?"[1]

Swamiji has given some valuable advice regarding healthy food habits. "Concentrated food should be taken. To fill the stomach with a large quantity of rice is the root of laziness."[2] "Take such food as is substantial and nutritious and at the same time easily digested. The food should be such as contains the greatest nutriment in the smallest compass, and be at the same time quickly assimilable...It is sufficient food to have rice, Daal (lentils), whole-wheat chapatis (unfermented bread), fish, vegetables

---

1. *Ibid.*, Vol.V, page 375.
2. *Ibid.*, Vol.V, page 375.

and milk."[1] He praised the eating habits of Japanese who took small frequent meals consisting of rice and soup of split peas.

Digestive disorders are extremely common among Indians and Swamiji rightly diagnosed their cause as faulty eating habits. "All fried things are really poisonous; in hot countries the less oil and clarified butter (ghee) taken, the better. Those who take fried food suffer from dyspepsia and ultimately the digestion is ruined. ...Spices are no food at all. To take them in abundance is only due to bad habit."[2] Another cause of diseases like diarrhoea, dysentery, cholera, typhoid fever, jaundice, etc. is eating unwashed or contaminated food. Appealing to the religious sense of devoted Hindus, Swamiji advised them to be as particular about avoiding *nimitta dosha* (physical uncleanliness) as they were about *aashraya dosha*, bad character of one who may be serving food. "The sweet vendor's shop is Death's door."[3] "It has become too

---

1. *Ibid.*, Vol.V, page 486.
2. *Ibid.*, Vol.V, page 486.
3. *Ibid.*, Vol.V, page 486.

common with us to buy food from the sweet vendor's shop in the bazaar, and you can judge for yourselves how impure these confections are from the point of view of *nimitta dosha*; for, being kept exposed, the dirt and dust of the roads as well as dead insects adhere to them, and how stale and polluted they must sometimes be."[1] Swamiji was against all fermented foods. "And as for fermented bread, it is also poison. Never take any fermented thing."[2] With the increasing variety of "fancy foods" and drinks now available in the market with very little food value, Swamiji's advice regarding food becomes all the more pertinent. If not heeded, we may witness more such scenes as an emaciated person clothed in rags sitting miserably in a city slum drinking five-rupee Coca Cola.

In *"The East and the West,"* Swamiji has discussed in detail about food and eating habits. After reviewing the various prevalent views about vegetarian and non-vegetarian diet, Swamiji gives his

---

1. *Ibid.*, Vol.V, page 481.
2. *Ibid.*, Vol.V, page 488.

considered opinion for the masses of a poor country like India, who have to struggle hard for survival. "He who has to steer the boat of his life with strenuous labour through the constant life and death struggles and competition of this world, must of necessity take meat. So long as there will be in human society such a thing as the triumph of the strong over the weak, animal food is required or some other substitute for it has to be discovered; otherwise the weak will naturally be crushed under the feet of the strong."[1]

Swamiji was no dietitian, but his observations and advice is most scientific and in accord with the rules of diet and health. It may be mentioned that in recent years soybean has been discovered as a vegetarian substitute for meat. It is rich in proteins and can be taken by those strict vegetarians who would not like to eat meat.

The next important causes of disease are drinking impure or polluted water, and unclean habits. "Impure water and impure

---

1. *Ibid.*, Vol.V, page 485.

food is the cause of all maladies."[1] To his brother disciples Swamiji advised, "Have two filters made and use that filtered water for both cooking and drinking purposes. Boil water before filtering. ...Keep a strict eye on everybody's health. ...Dirty clothes are the chief cause of disease."[2]

Intermarriage and Early Marriage of Girls

Swami Vivekananda pointed out that marriages confined within a single caste and early marriage of girls were important causes of physical weakness of the offspring. "There is, for example, a good cause for intermarriage in India, in the absence of which the race is becoming physically weaker day by day"[3] "...and for this very reason the race is getting deteriorated physically, and consequently all sorts of diseases and other evils are finding a ready entrance into it!... The blood having had to circulate within the narrow circle of a limited number of individuals has been vitiated, so the new-born

---

1. *Ibid.*, Vol. V, page 489.
2. *Ibid.*, Vol. VI, page 333.
3. *Ibid.*, Vol. V, page 334.

children inherit from their very birth the constitutional diseases of their fathers... their bodies have very little power to resist the microbes of any disease."[1] For similar reasons Swamiji criticized severely the practice of child marriage. "Somehow the parents must dispose off a girl in marriage if she be nine or ten years of age! And what a rejoicing of the whole family if a child is born to her at the age of thirteen!"[2]

Something for All

Let us now study the sociological ideas of Swami Vivekananda, and their implications for the national health policy. Swamiji was a patriot with the practical wisdom of a sociologist and social scientist, and his teachings have great relevance for the sociology of medicine. He said, "We want the greatest possible good from the least outlay."[3] Translated into modern terms, it would mean adopting the most cost-effective methods. He did not favour any reform

1. *Ibid.*, Vol. V, page 340-41.
2. *Ibid.*, Vol. V, page 343.
3. *Ibid.*, Vol. VII, 1979, page 509.

which would benefit only a limited section of society. "All that you mean by your social reform," he said, "is either widow remarriage or female emancipation, or something of that sort. Do you not? And these again are directed within the confines of a few of the castes only. Such a scheme of reform may do good to a few, no doubt, but of what avail is that to the whole nation? Is that reform or only a form of selfishness, somehow to cleanse your own room and keep it tidy and let others go from bad to worse!"[1] "Most of what you talk of social reform does not touch the poor masses."[2] He was indeed bitter towards those who thought that "for the luxury of a handful of rich, let millions of men and women remain submerged in the hell of want and abysmal depth of ignorance, for if they get wealth and education (and health) society will be upset!"[3] The state of affairs, he said, must be just the reverse.

"If there is inequality in nature, still there must be equal chances for all, or if greater

1. *Ibid.*, Vol. V, page 333-34.
2. *Ibid.*, Vol. V, page 334.
3. *Ibid.*, Vol. V, page 146.

for some and for some less, the weaker should be given more chance than the strong. ... If the son of a brahmin needs one teacher, that of a *chandala* [the neglected low-caste person] needs ten. For greater help must be given to him whom nature has not endowed with an acute intellect from birth."[1]

We have noted that the modern western model of high-tech medical care is extremely expensive and elite-oriented. "In a developing country [like India], the fortunate rich urban elite have access to almost any highly sophisticated technology, either in the capital or abroad, while many of the rural poor have no modern medical health care whatever."[2] Such a state of affairs Swamiji would condemn as selfishness. Emphasis must be to provide something for everyone, rather than to give more to the already fortunate few.

The following chart[3] shows the percentage of population having health

---

1. *Ibid.*, Vol. V, page 319.

2. King, M.H., *"Medicine in an Unjust World"*; *Oxford Textbook of Medicine*, ELBS (London: Oxford Univ. Press, 1985), p. 3.9.

3. King (*Ibid.*), p. 3.7.

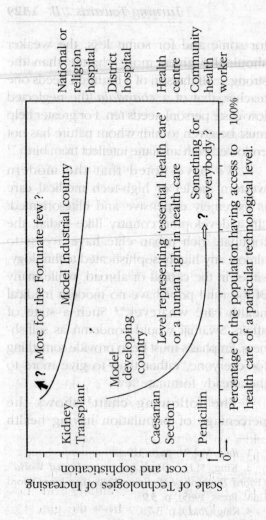

Scale of Technologies of increasing cost and sophistication

Kidney Transplant

Caesarian Section

Penicillin

More for the Fortunate few ?

Model Industrial country

Model developing country

Level representing 'essential health care' or a human right in health care

Something for everybody ?

Percentage of the population having access to health care of a particular technological level.

0   100%

National or religion hospital

District hospital

Health centre

Community health worker

care at a particular technological level in a model industrial country and in a model developing one. The black and white arrows represent policy choices in the deployment of resources. It is obvious that development in the direction of the white arrow would be in line with the directives of Swami Vivekananda. In the figure, a level of basic "human right" or primary health care can be inserted below "penicillin". In a poor country like India where resources are scarce, it is far more advisable to provide pure drinking water, healthy food, and assistance of trained dai for every mother during delivery of her child, rather than facilities for kidney transplant or coronary bypass surgery.

In this context it may be mentioned that Swamiji believed in working at the micro-level, at the level of the individual citizen. For, he had great faith in the average, poor Indian whom he considered the builder of a New India. "Let her [the New India]," he said, "arise—out of the peasant's cottage, grasping the plough; out of the huts of the fisherman, the cobbler, and the sweeper. Let her spring from the grocer's shop, from beside the oven of the fritter seller…"[1] The doctor, the compounder, the nurse, the village health worker, the village dai, are all builders of New India. Health, medical care, and health education must reach every Indian—the peasants, the labourers, the fishermen, the cobblers and the sweepers!

Swami Vivekananda was never tired of reminding that "the nation lives in the cottages."[2] He was against urbanization and shifting of youth from the villages to the cities. Instead, he wanted the city youth to go to the villages and educate the villagers who cannot come to the centres of education. He also said that longevity increases by staying in the villages and diseases are almost unknown there.[3] This is enough of a hint for us to know that Swamiji would have preferred emphasis on primary health

1. *The Complete Works of Swami Vivekananda*, Vol. VII, page 327.

2. *Ibid.*, Vol. V, page 29.

3. *The Life of Swami Vivekananda by His Eastern and Western Disciples*, (Calcutta: Advaita Ashrama, 1983) Vol. I, pp.274-75.

centres in the villages over the modern medical centres in the cities "which look more like airports than therapeutic environments," and where patients tend to feel helpless and frightened.[1]

Against Blindly Imitating the West

There is a trend in medicine to follow the USA in everything, almost blindly. The current prestige of high technology medicine is such that it dominates the ambition of the medical profession. Swami Vivekananda was extremely critical of the "terrible mania of becoming westernized."[2] "Alas, to such a state is our country reduced! People will look upon their own gold as brass while the brass of the foreigner is gold to them."[3] "I am so thoroughly against every affectation of the western ideas…what a frippery civilization it is indeed that the foreigners have brought over here. What a materialistic illusion have they created!"[4]

---

1. Capra, Fritjof, *The Turning Point* (New York: Flamingo, 1989) page 148.
2. *The Complete Works of Swami Vivekananda*, Vol. V, page 372.
3. *Ibid.*, Vol. V, page 373.
4. *Ibid.*, Vol. VI, page 319.

Although the sophisticated high-tech medicine is prestigious and capable, it is not universal, or is rather only partially universal, being too expensive and beyond the reach of the poor. Not to accept it, or to refuse to plan one's services according to it may mean getting labelled "technically inadequate", or feeling medically inferior, or socially deviant. To follow the call of Swamiji and to go against such a powerful trend requires considerable courage. But we must be bold to mould our medical services to suit the dire needs of Indian villages and slums rather than imitate the technological sophistry of the USA.

"Appropriate" technology for the poor does not mean cheap or primitive technology, but scientifically sound procedures in materials and methods which are practical in society and effective. The use of bifid inoculation needles for smallpox vaccination, which paved the way to its eradication, use of oral rehydration fluid for diarrhoea, monthly weight records of infants and children to monitor their growth— are all parts of appropriate technology and are equally scientific and far more pertinent than the use of fibre-optic endo-scopes, ultrasound machines, computer tomography or micro-surgery.

One of the reasons why Swamiji was against blind acceptance of Western norms and methods was their tendency to become exploitative. In the beginning Swamiji was charmed by the ability of Americans to quickly form organizations, but he soon realized that such organizations in the heat of competition could behave "like packs of wolves, without any beauty," and exploit the simple and the poor. It is unfortunate that this unhealthy western trend is gradu-ally permeating such a noble profession as the medical. Taking the lead from Swamiji, every effort must be made to keep it free from such unethical trends.

What about specialization and "super-specialization" which has formed an inte-gral part of modern medicine? Although it was not developed to such a degree during Swamiji's time, it seems that he would not have favoured it. He has hinted that a broad-based person, combining various skills in his single personality, was better suited for Indian conditions. He once told his disciples:

"You must be prepared to go into deep meditation now and the next moment you must be ready to go and cultivate these fields. You must be prepared to explain the difficult intricacies of the shastras now and the next moment to go and sell the produce of the field in the market. You must be prepared for all menial services, not only here, but elsewhere also."[1]

Translated into medical terms, we need doctors who could read an E.C.G., put a scalp vein drip, repair a hernia, set a fractured bone, pass an endo-tracheal tube, detect an amoeba under the microscope, and teach medical assistants competently, rather than a doctor who specializes in diseases of one organ in one age group, or does only one operation, or who can pass an endoscope through only one orifice. It may be mentioned here that Mrs. Indira Gandhi exhorted Indian doctors not to become too specialized.[2]

From the foregoing it must not be concluded that Swamiji was against

---

1. *Ibid.*, Vol. III, page 447.

2. King, *"Medicine in an Unjust World"*, p 3.9.

scientific methods or scientific advancement. He preferred allopathic medicine because it was backed by experimentation. He had himself undergone various types of treatments: allopathic, magnetic, ayurvedic, etc. He wanted that experimentations be done in other systems of medicine also.

Education

Swamiji suggested education as the chief weapon for the regeneration of India. "Educate the masses by going from door to door, and make them realize their pitiable condition."[1] Along with material help, Swamiji also wanted preaching to be done because, "all the wealth of the world cannot help one little Indian village if the people are not taught to help themselves."[2] Education which would teach people to be self-reliant and frugal, that is what he wanted.[3] By education he did not mean only moral and spiritual education, but also education in the secular subjects, like

1. *The Complete Works*, Vol. V, page 380.
2. *Ibid.*, Vol. VII, page 507-8.
3. *Ibid.*, Vol. VII, page 508.

geography,[1] chemistry, physics, and especially physiology.[2] It seems Swamiji had a special fascination for physiology and medical science.

Indian masses must therefore be made competent to take care of their own medical needs. Fundamentals of health and sanitation, first-aid, and preliminary treatment of many maladies can be easily taught to the people. Spread of diseases and the out-break of epidemics can never be prevented unless the masses are informed about the way they occur and the means of preventing them.

Swamiji was a strong advocate of religious as well as secular education for women, "which would be of benefit not only to them, but to others as well..."[3] and with which they will solve their own problems.[4] The health of the baby largely depends upon the health of the mother

---

1. *Ibid.*, Vol. V, page 288.
2. *Ibid.*, Vol. VII, page 507.
3. *Ibid.*, Vol. V, page 343.
4. *Ibid.*, Vol. V, page 342.

and on how hygienically and healthily she takes care of the child.

Three Steps of Help

It is said that if one is planning for one year, let him grow a crop; if for thirty years, plant trees; and if for a hundred years, then let it be man-making. Similarly, three levels can be recognized in medicare. Curative medicine is short term; preventive medicine and health education come under the second category, while the scheme of man-making alone can bring lasting results. It was this third step which was emphasized by Swami Vivekananda.

Swamiji also recognized three levels of service, viz., the physical and material, the intellectual, and the spiritual.[1] Medical treatment falls under the category of physical help. Health education is the intellectual help, which is important if the benefits of physical help are to be sustained. The most important is spiritual help, which alone can permanently cure the disease of worldliness. Swamiji was a spiritual giant and a spiritual physician par-excellence. Indeed, he has

1. *Ibid.*, Vol. I, 1984, page 53.

advised his disciples to carry out all the three types of healings, depending upon the person or persons and conditions they were dealing with. He has thus, in a way, advocated a comprehensive holistic medicine. There is no aspect of health which has been left out by Swamiji.

Conclusion

Let us now summarize Swami Vivekananda's advice for health and his message for the medical world. He advised the sick to get over their suffering by asserting their divine nature. The doctors and health workers must serve the patients as God. Wholesome food, pure drinking water and clean habits are necessary to prevent common diseases. Girls in particular must get health education and must not be married too young. National health must be planned in such a way that the masses, particularly those living in the villages, get basic health care. Let not the western methods of treatment be imitated blindly; they must be modified according to our needs. Health education must be spread to the masses so that people can look after their own health-care needs. And finally, let character be formed, and doctors equipped with various skills go from village to village and serve the poor masses.

Seventy-eight years later in 1978 the Alma-Ata Conference suggested comprehensive primary health care as the most hopeful solution for "Health for all by the year 2000." "Primary health care includes at least education concerning the prevailing health problems and the methods of preventing and controlling them, the promotion of adequate food supply and proper nutrition, together with a sufficient supply of safe water and basic sanitation. It also includes maternal and child health, family planning, and immunization against the major infectious diseases, as well as prevention and control of locally endemic diseases and injuries, and the provision of essential drugs."[1] Did not this declaration of Alma-Ata, in part read like the message of Swami Vivekananda? However, it lacked the man-making message and the spiritual dimension.

---

1. King, *"Medicine in an Unjust World"*, p.3.9.

Values for All-round Health

$\mathcal{H}$ealth is a neglected entity not only at the national level, where only 2% of the national financial outlay is allotted to health, but also at the personal level. Most of us are not careful about observing the rules of health. It is surprising, therefore, that we do not fall ill more often. The reason is that the human physiological and psychological systems have a tremendous capacity for adjustment and re-adjustment. We have an inbuilt system of stress-resistance, an effective inherent mechanism for fighting the external onslaughts of disease factors. So we fall ill only when the attack is really severe. This is, again, one of the reasons why we do not worry about health. We simply take it for granted. This should not be so. Every one must have at least some basic knowledge about the rules of health and the values associated with it.

What is Health?

But what is health? Traditionally, health is defined as absence of disease and this working definition is accepted by most citizens and even doctors, whose task is to repair the human biological machine when it breaks down. However, this concept does not explain major problems of health like malnutrition, accidents, drug-abuse, mental disease, etc. So there is a better definition given by WHO: 'Health is a state of complete, physical, mental and social well-being and not merely absence of disease.' But health is not merely 'a state,' it is 'a process of continuous equilibrium of body-form and function, which results from successful dynamic adjustment to forces tending to disturb it.' Again, there are grades of health: positive health, i.e., cent percent fitness expected of high-class athletes; better health, in well-nourished people; freedom from illness, in average individuals; unrecognized illness and mild illness in malnourished people.

One of the first tasks for us is to recognize where we stand in this spectrum of health.

Values for Physical Health

Let us now see what values and which factors govern health. They are, in short, (1) diet, (2) exercise, and (3) rest and sleep. Moderation in these three and avoidance of extremes is the secret of keeping the body healthy. Do not stuff your stomach with too much food either during the day or during the night. It is advisable to take light food at night and reduce the quantity of food to at least three quarters if not half, after the age of 40. There is a good advice given by Ayurveda: Fill half the stomach with food, one quarter with water, and keep the remaining quarter empty for movement of air.

Of course, there would be exceptions. After working the whole day a labourer would like to stuff his stomach well with food at night. The Western custom of a heavy dinner is unhealthy, while the Jain custom of not eating after sunset is very good. Some people take frequent small meals. Others take only one or two principal meals a day. The general rule is, do not remain hungry longer than six hours, and keep at least a three-hour gap between two intakes of food. However, no hard and fast rules can be made, except that one must observe moderation. An occasional one-day fasting or a half-day fasting is good. There is an adage in traditional circles: *langhanam paramam aushadham,* 'fasting is the best medicine.'

No hard and fast rules can be made, again, as to the quality or type of food. That food is best for us which we are used to from our childhood. And it must be balanced, i.e., the proportion of proteins, fats and carbohydrates must be proper. The food must also be easily digestible. Now, if we observe the food habits of people in different parts of India, we will find vast differences. But surprisingly we will find that the proportion of these three constituents, viz. proteins, fats and carbohydrates, is maintained even though people are not taught anything about it. But the poor suffer from malnutrition in general, while the affluent suffer from the problems created by overeating. Foods are often fried because it makes them tasty, but it must be remembered that fried fats are more difficult to digest than unfried fats.

Other values for a healthy body are rest and exercise. Five to seven hours of sleep is generally enough, but as I said, here also there are no hard and fast rules. Young people sleep more soundly, while as the age advances, we get less and less sound sleep and it is less refreshing. Yoga postures (*asanas*) are excellent means of physical and mental relaxation. But apart from yoga postures, brisk physical exercise must also be done every day regularly. This is very important.

Apart from these basic values for physical health, there are certain precautions which one must observe to avoid falling ill. One important value is cleanliness. Be very careful about taking clean, pure, filtered water and also clean food, with clean hands. Three-fourths of the diseases in India are produced due to uncleanliness. These are called food-borne and water-borne diseases. There are also diseases due to mosquitoes, dust and pollution. One must protect oneself from these. Then there is a large group of diseases caused by psychological factors. Every type of excitement—anger, emotional, sexual, etc. as also anxiety, depression, etc., leads to stimulation of the autonomic nervous system, which can cause diseases like hypertension, coronary artery disease, peptic ulcer, etc. So one must be careful.

Mental Health

Today mental illness has become far more widespread than physical illness. According to a 1942 report, in USA one out of every twenty persons goes to a mental hospital at least once in his or her lifetime. And this number has increased with the passage of time. Social psychologist Erich Fromm has written a book titled *The Sane Society*. He begins with giving statistics of prevalent crime rate—thefts, murders, rapes, etc.—in USA and concludes that the whole society has become insane. He says that we are living not in a mentally healthy or sane society but in an insane society. His observation is very true. The unfortunate thing is that this fact is not generally recognized. Even if others think that a particular person is mentally unhealthy, in most cases the individual concerned would not accept it. How can people get well unless they recognize and accept their disease and approach a doctor?

But what do we mean by mental health? We can define mental health this way: 'A balanced and undisturbed state of mind, not only during favourable conditions but even during mentally stressful condition.' A very good word for it is *samata*, or *samatva*, which is elaborated in the *Gita*. Mental stress could be of two types: acute and chronic or sustained. Seeing the two armies arrayed for war, with relatives on both sides, is an example of acute psychological stress for Arjuna, under whose weight he succumbed and showed signs of neurosis like trembling of limbs, perspiration, reeling of head, etc. Banishment into forest for fourteen years is an example of chronic psychological stress for Rama, who bore it commendably without breaking down.

Now, mental illness and health can also have various grades. Positive health would mean not to break down under any type of psychological stress, no matter how intense, whether it comes in the form of temptation, threat, pain, fear, or suffering. Most of us cannot fulfill this condition and cannot claim to have positive mental health. We often break down temporarily under sorrow and stress if it is too severe, but soon recover our mental poise. This is the second grade of mental health. The third grade would be when a person remains anxious or depressed, and continues to feel inner disturbance, but it does not express in his or her behaviour and day-to-day activity. Most of the people fall into this category. There are those who require regular use of tranquillizers and/or anti-depressants and alcohol to keep up their inner and external poise. And, finally, there are those whose behaviour pattern is altered so much that they need to be hospitalized in a mental institution.

The aspect of mental health just described deals mainly with an individual's reaction to external or internal stress situation. But there is another aspect which concerns the harmonious development and working of the various faculties of an individual. We have emotions and sentiments, desires and drives; we have our will as well as the intellect. All these mental faculties of thinking, feeling and willing must be harmonized together, otherwise we will 'think' something and 'will' something else.

We may want to do something, but our intellect may suggest that we must not do it. The ideal mental health would in this context mean the fullest and, at the same time, harmonious development of all the mental faculties. According to Swami Vivekananda, Buddha was the sanest person, mentally the healthiest person, ever born. He had a large and feeling heart, which could feel even for the suffering animals and yet he was not sentimental. He was an intellectual giant and yet did not get lost into the net of mere argumentation. He was intensely active and yet had perfect control over his mind and senses.

Values for Mental Health

How do we get an ideal mental health? Here are some hints as to the means and values one must cultivate. I would call them 4Ds: Discrimination, Detachment, Devotion, and Discipline. These will develop, strengthen and integrate intellect or thinking, action or willing, feeling or emotions, and our senses respectively. Let us take them up one by one.

Discrimination includes reasoning, observation, critical assessment of an event or object, and an analytical study of any specific thing. Now, if we are able to practise philosophical discrimination between the real and the unreal, if we carefully and critically analyse our own real nature and that of the world around, we may obtain direct insight into the true nature of our own Self *(atman)* and, like Ramana Maharshi, can get fully established in the Self. We will then be *svastha*, which is the real meaning of the term 'health'. Even short of this highest state, we can make good use of our discriminating faculty and get at the depth of the events of life, and this is a great gain so far as mental health and stability are concerned.

Next, detachment. One of the major causes of mental instability and suffering is attachment to persons, places, things and specific type of activity. We seek fruits of actions, and when our expectations are frustrated, we get upset and lose our mental poise. We must practise detachment. We must be more objective in our approach, not only towards the events of the external world, but also towards the events occurring in our mental world.

Devotion integrates, strengthens and develops our emotions. We have hundreds of emotions which drive us in different directions. Devotion to God, to one's guru, or to a scripture, even to an ideal, is a great stabilizing force. Faith, dedication, etc. are its various aspects. One of the causes of failing mental health among people is the gradual decline and weakening of faith. Faith is a tremendous sustaining force against various types of challenges. If one does not like to have faith and devotion to a deity, one may have them for an ideal, a principle. There is nothing wrong in it. As a matter of fact, psychologically speaking, faith in God or a prophet ultimately boils down to faith in some ideals.

Finally, there must be discipline in all its aspects. The body must be disciplined, the senses must be controlled, and must obey the commands of the mind. The mind too must be disciplined. Just as a chariot with disciplined and controlled horses, with tight reins in the hands of an expert driver reaches the goal safely without meeting with accidents, so also a disciplined body with disciplined senses, mind and intellect conduces to the overall well-being of the individual. The eight-fold path of yoga with meditation as the central theme is essentially a scheme of all-round discipline.

These values represented by the 4D's must be practiced everyday without break for a long time and with great earnestness. Mere intellectual understanding is not enough. Our goal is to build sound mental health. Just as for sound physical health we need to do regular exercise and have a nutritious diet everyday, so also these 4D's must be practised everyday for sound mental health. Just as our physical body needs a balanced and nutritious diet, the mind too needs a healthy mental food. Again, as in the case of gross food, we are extremely careless about our mental food too. I mean the thoughts and ideas which we get from our senses, the scenes that we see, the books that we read, the company that we keep, and the thoughts that we think. Relishing crime and sex in TV serials, reading vulgar, trash literature, we cannot hope to have a healthy mind. It is better to live alone than to live in the company of

fools or of people with criminal or immoral
tendencies. Such people are psychologically
sick, and mental sickness is more contagious
than physical sickness. Seek the company
of sane or mentally healthy people and of
holy people.

Just as we need physical rest and sleep
for physical health, we need mental rest,
recreation and relaxation for mental health.
Most people are not able to relax mentally;
they are not able to get over their worries
and anxieties. So they take sleeping-pills
or resort to alcohol. That does not solve the
problem; it rather makes it more complicated. Modern psychologists have suggested
a number of ways of relaxing mentally.
Music has great recreational and relaxing
value. Devotional music is elevating too.
Rhythmic chanting of a mantra has similar
value. Guided practice of Yoga-nidra, as
advocated by the Bihar School of Yoga is
also very effective.

In the context of mental health and
mental diseases, let us see what Tulsidas
has said in his *Ramacharit Manas*. In the
Uttar-kanda, under the section popularly
known as *'Manas Roga'* or Mental Diseases,

he says that ignorance is the root of all mental diseases. Lust, greed and anger are compared to increased *vata, pitta* and *kapha,* and when these combine, they lead to delirium. Sense desires form a different set of ailments. Attachment is eczema, aversion is itch, elation and depression are the diseases of the throat, envy at seeing someone else's prosperity is tuberculosis. Thus, as a matter of fact, evil tendencies are mental diseases and the different rules and regulations, codes of conduct, moral virtues, etc. are the remedies.

A major cause of mental ill-health is our faulty reaction to persons and situations, which is often tarnished by envy, anger, jealousy or hatred. This must be avoided by cultivating friendship towards the happy and prosperous, compassion towards those who suffer, a feeling of positive joy towards the virtuous, and indifference towards the wicked. This fourfold mental attitude conduces to mental peace and health, and is the basis for all sane social conduct.

Regular practice of rhythmic breathing too helps in achieving physical and mental health. According to Hindu psychology, the *pranamaya-kosha* is situated between the *annamaya* and the *manomaya-kosha* and is therefore affected by, and in turn influences, both the *koshas*. In other words, breathing is influenced by mental and physical states, and it influences both mind and body. Hence its regulation by practice of rhythmic breathing conduces to physical and mental health.

Social Health and Disease

No account of values for health can be complete without reference to social health. It is true that we as individuals can contribute substantially to the health of the society by ourselves becoming physically and mentally healthy, since every one of us is a part of society. But it is equally true that the social health affects the individual, and efforts must be made to improve the social health. The ecology of health is a study of the relation between variations in the environment and our state of health. From this standpoint health is defined as a state of dynamic equilibrium between people and their environment. It has been recognized that the control of diseases by environmental manipulation is much cheaper, safer, effective, and rational than treatment of individual cases. Thus there are social, cultural and psychological factors related to health. It is not possible to raise the level of people's health without changing their social environment, living habits, and culturally acquired unhealthy practices.

In recent years, a new concept of holistic health has evolved. This concept recognizes the strength of social, economic, environmental, and even political influences on health. Health is now recognized as a multidimensional and inter sectorial process. It is now an integral part of development and is the essence of productive life. It involves individual, group, state and international responsibility. That health is a worldwide social goal had been highlighted by the launching of the WHO movement called 'Health for All by the Year 2000.' The World Assembly referred to it as 'the attainment by all the people of the world to a level of health that will permit them to lead a socially and economically productive life.' Health for all posed new challenges before the medical world and the governments of various countries. Now even conscientious citizens cannot remain content with taking care of only their own health and observing their own rules of health and hygiene, and neglecting other people.

The signs of social ill-health can be seen everywhere. Let us go out of our limited sphere of activity and observe the masses living in slums, or the crowded quarters of a city, or in the nearby village, or let us peep into the crowded outdoor of a government general hospital. The scene which we shall see will convince us of the appalling poverty and malnutrition prevailing in the country. During his travels as a wandering monk through the length and breadth of our country, Swami Vivekananda was stunned by the extent of poverty, malnutrition and even starvation prevalent among Indian masses. This getting introduced to the socioeconomic problem of health is the first step. After this, let us act in whichever way each of us can. May be one of us can contribute only to the extent of treating the anaemia of one of the poor, suffering from nutritional anaemia. Another may like to form a group or association and raise funds and treat the labourers living in a slum. Still others may like to give health education to the masses and teach them the importance of cleanliness, etc. There might be some who may not be able to act, but they must at least think globally.

To think of others first, to feel for the suffering humanity, and to serve them is probably the best way to gain one's own mental health. Serving the sick, the poor, the hungry, considering them the veritable embodiments of God integrates our personality and helps us to manifest our inner potentialities as nothing else can. Service, therefore, must form an integral and indispensable part of any scheme for physical and mental health.

Even those who are not able to serve others in a positive and active way may practise these virtues which have a bearing upon social life. Let us not hurt others through thought, word or deed. Let us not cheat others or steal something which lawfully belongs to someone else. Let us not hoard too many things. Let us try to live on the bare minimum, because every extra object we possess is depriving someone else of its use. In this context, the example of an American lady called Peace Pilgrim is worth remembering. When this lady was in her twenties she got divinely inspired and gave away all her possessions, except the bare minimum which included a pant, a shirt and a tunic, a comb and some stationery material, a pair of socks and shoes. Her reasoning was that she ought not to have anything more than what she needed because there are millions living under the bare necessity line. She then travelled on foot all over USA as a messenger of peace. She would rest wherever she got shelter— under the trees, on the footpath, on the railway station and bus stations, or in homes when invited. She would eat when offered food. And she was one of the healthiest ladies both physically and mentally. We need not imitate her literally. But let us take her spirit. Let us try to do what little sacrifice we can for others or to see in what little way we can serve and help them.

Some medical philosophers have in recent times started talking of spiritual health, and this word has even appeared in one of the textbooks of preventive medicine. Holistic Health and Holistic Medicine have, of course, become quite popular terms. The latest introduction into the vocabulary of health is Quantum Health. However, this much can be safely asserted that if we follow the rules of physical and mental health, observe moral and ethical values, and contribute toward social health by service, our spiritual unfoldment is bound to occur. Spiritual health is nothing occult or secret.

The ultimate aim is to attain spiritual health, to be established in one's own spiritual nature, or to realize our true Self (*atman*). Once that is attained, nothing more remains to be obtained at the levels of physical and mental health. Sri Ramakrishna was so well established, *svastha* in his Self, that he never cared for physical health and did not bother about the cancer of the throat. He, however, did not resist being treated by doctors. There are other instances of saints who did not even treat their fatal illnesses. One Jain nun had cancer of the breast. But she bore all the pain and suffering for two years with perfect equanimity without consenting to treatment.

Conclusion

We have discussed some of the many values and guidelines to develop a healthy body, a healthy mind, and a healthy society. One may or may not follow them. As has been said, there are various grades of health. One may pull on, as most of us do, with minimum health. But for excellence in any field of life, perfect health is essential. Health is an indispensable human resource. It is the very foundation of success in any sphere of life. To achieve perfect health, we must observe a daily routine of healthy activities and endeavours to develop healthy habits. Habit formation—I mean, *good* habits—is laborious and time-consuming while it is very easy to acquire bad habits. Let us get up early in the morning, at least half an hour before sunrise; practise concentration of mind, do regular exercise, keep our room and belongings neat, clean and tidy. Let us behave with decency, dignity and modesty with others; take every opportunity to serve others. Read noble, healthy, elevating literature and be in good company. Let us be punctual and trustworthy. These and many other values should be cultivated for a healthy body and mind so that one can lead a long, active and productive life.[1]

---

1. Talk delivered in a youth convention.

My God the Sick – The Sevashrama Movement

$\mathscr{S}$wami Vivekananda's following oft-quoted words are well known:

May I be born again and again, and suffer thousands of miseries, so that I may worship the only God that exists, the only God I believe in, the sum total of all souls— and above all, my God the wicked, my God the miserable, my God the poor of all races, of all species, is the special object of my worship.

On another occasion he said:

You have read *matridevo bhava, pitridevo bhava*—look upon your mother as God, look upon your father as God— but I say *daridradevo bhava, murkhadevo bhava*...The poor, the illiterate, the ignorant, the afflicted—let these be your God. Know that service to these alone is the highest religion.

While Swamiji has not mentioned 'My God the Sick' or *rogi devo bhava*, the idea is implied in the word 'poor' and 'miserable'. In fact Swamiji wanted to start an *annasatra* and a Sevashrama (Home of Service) on the southern portion of the Belur Math. However, this desire of his was fulfilled, not in exactly the way he envisaged, but in a much grander way— in what can be called the *Sevashrama Movement.*

The first Sevashrama to come up was at Varanasi. On June 1900, Jaminiranjan, a young man, was winding his way before dawn through one of the narrow, dingy lanes of Varanasi, leading to the bathing ghat. A groan from a feeble human throat fell into his ear. Many had already passed that way, but none had stopped to look sideways to investigate. But Jaminiranjan stopped and found an old lady, ill and starved, lying on the road side. As he approached her, she said feebly, 'I have not taken anything for four days, my son, give me some food.' Jaminiranjan lifted the lady and laid her carefully on the verandah of the nearby house and rushed to the bathing ghat and begged a four anna coin from the first gentleman he met. He purchased some cooked food and fed the old lady and thus saved her life. Thus was sown the seed of dedicated service of God in the form of the poor and the suffering which was to grow into a mighty banyan tree of a large institution that would render service to thousands of needy.

This old lady was one of the many religious people who come to spend their last days in the holy city of Kashi—the *mukti kshetra*—and who are reduced to a state of dire poverty and helplessness due to the ruthlessness of man and the irony of fate.

After rendering this emergency help to her, Jaminiranjan went to his friends Haridas, Charu chandra (later Swami Shubhananda), Kedarnath (later Swami Achalananda) and others and gave them an account of what had happened. A band of youth with Charuchandra as the leader had already formed a study circle with an aim to realizing God in the light of the teachings of Sri Ramakrishna and Swami Vivekananda. They collected donations and managed to admit the lady to a hospital. The young group now decided upon the future action: service to the poor, the needy, the destitute and the sick; and organized themselves into an association and named it 'Home of relief'. They searched for the needy on the road sides, in lanes and by-lanes and arranged for their relief by sending some to the hospital and giving food and clothing to others. A patient of typhoid fever was the first indoor patient who was housed in Kedarnath's house and was nursed by others. Soon the need for a spacious accommodation for indoor patients was felt and a small house for Rs.5 per month was rented. A small out-door homeopathic dispensary was also started. One room was for indoor patients, and the dispensary was also the office and the bed-room of the two whole-time workers—Charuchandra and Jaminiranjan.

Soon the enthusiasm, dedication and indefatigable labour of the youth attracted the attention and sympathy of the prominent citizens, on whose advice the first general meeting of the association was held on 5th September 1900, in which it was renamed, 'The Poor Men's Relief

Association'. Within six months the indoor and outdoor work increased so much that a more spacious house at Dashaswamedh Road had to be rented which was later shifted to a bigger house in Ramapura in 1901. Within eighteen months 330 men and 334 women received some kind of relief or the other.

In February 1902 Swami Vivekananda visited Varanasi. He was highly pleased by the work done by the association. However, he advised them to change the name to 'Home of Service', for, as he said, 'Who are you to render relief? You can only serve. The pride of rendering relief leads to ruin... How arrogant it is on the part of a man to think another lower and humbler than himself? Service—and not mercy should be your guiding principle—service to man, the image of God.' He turned to Charuchandra and said, 'Regard every pice collected for the poor as your life blood. Such noble work can be carried on properly and permanently by those only who have renounced everything.' Swamiji wrote an appeal to the public on behalf of the Home of Service, which accompanied the first report of the

Home, in 1902. Swamiji also instructed Swami Brahmananda to keep a watch on the organization. With the latter's approval and by a resolution of the managing committee of the Home of Service, the association was affiliated to the Ramakrishna Mission and came to be known by its present name, 'Ramakrishna Mission Home of Service', on September 23, 1903.

Things moved fast thereafter. Unexpected donations from two donors and equally unexpected offer of a plot of land for a paltry Rs.6000/- enabled the Home to have a place of its own on which Swami Brahmananda laid the first foundation stone of the future building on 16th April 1908. Swami Vijnanananda was the chief architect and the new building was inaugurated by Swami Brahmananda on 16th May 1910. The Holy Mother visited the Home of Service on 8th November 1912 and having been taken round, was extremely delighted and exclaimed: 'Thakur himself lives here and Goddess Laxmi has chosen this place as her abode.' The ten rupee currency note donated by her is still preserved as a sacred treasure and blessing in the Home.

Let us now review the events occurring almost simultaneously at Kankhal. Swami Vivekananda, who, from personal experience knew the helpless condition of monks living at Haridwar and nearby places, told Swami Kalyanananda: 'My boy, can you do something for the ailing monks at Haridwar and Rishikesh? There is none to look after them when they fall ill. Go and serve them.' In June 1901 Kalyanananda began his work at Kankhal, a village near Haridwar. Two rooms were hired at Rs.3/- per month which served as his dispensary, indoor ward, bed room, office and everything and his stock of medicines was contained in a box. Living on alms, the Swami distributed medicines, not only to those who came to him, but also to those who could not, or would not stir out of their huts by visiting him. He was soon joined by Swami Nischayananda, another disciple of Swami Vivekananda. Ignoring physical hardship the twin-monks conducted a dispensary at Rishikesh, which was like a branch centre fifteen miles from Kankhal—walking all the way to and fro every day. Apart from treating monks in their huts, they would also perform the last rites of those monks who had died in their huts with none to perform these rites. They did not restrict their medical service to the monks only, but extended it to the untouchables and the so called outcasts. As a result, on the one hand they were castigated as untouchables— 'bhangis'—themselves, by the majority of the orthodox monks of the twin towns of Rishikesh and Haridwar, while on the other hand, they were highly respected by some others of whom Mandaleswar Swami Dhanraj Giri was the foremost. Once it so happened that in one Sadhu bhandara—a feast for monks—hosted at one of the maths, the 'outcasted monks' Kalyanananda and Nischayananda were not invited. When Mandaleswar Dhanraj Giri, the chief guest, learnt this, he rebuked the orthodox monks and said that these two monks were truly practising the Vedantic tenets of 'all is Brahman', and unless they were invited and honoured he would not accept hospitality. This opened the eyes of the orthodox monks and their antagonism towards the two monks ended.

This dedicated service soon attracted the attention of people and help started flowing in from various quarters. A plot of land was purchased in 1903 and the first building of two blocks, designed by Swami Vijnanananda, was constructed over it, and the Sevashrama was shifted to its new premises in 1905. In 1911 another ward of twenty beds was added and a Tuberculosis block was inaugurated in 1913. By the end of 1922 the number of beds had risen to 66.

It needs no mention that the work of service was wholly free and was supported by charity and donations which ranged from meagre four annas to thousand rupees or more. The monks sustained themselves by madhukari-bhiksha—begging food from door-to-door. Two others, Swami Japananda and Brahmachari Suren also went for bhiksha and thus reduced the burden on the sevashrama. However, there were practical difficulties involved in simultaneous begging and managing the affairs of the hospital. Realizing this, Swami Saradananda, the then General Secretary of the Mission, intervened and on his instruction eventually in 1921 the tradition of bhiksha was given up for greater efficiency. But both Kalyanananda and Nischayananda regretted for being deprived of the splendid freedom of begging.

The next Sevashrama to come up was at Vrindaban, where there was no facility for treatment of the multitude of pilgrims. In January 1907, taking their cue from the activities at Varanasi Sevashrama, some local people organized themselves to start a sevashrama, of whom Jajneswar Chandra and his son were the central figures. They were joined by Brahmachari Harendra of the Belur Math. The Sevashrama was initially located in the outer portion of Kalababu's Kunja, the ancestral property of Balaram Bose, where the patients were accommodated. The management passed onto the Mission on January 12, 1908, and in 1912 the number of indoor beds had gone up from four to fifteen. A plot of land measuring 8.32 acres was secured in 1915 on which a temporary structure was constructed so as to shift the Sevashrama from Kalababu's Kunj. Gradually a male and a female ward were constructed.

The next sevashrama to come up was at Allahabad in 1908 followed by many others: Lucknow (1914), Cortai (1913),

Bankura (1917), Sonargaon, Dhaka (1915), Garbeta, Midnapur, etc.

These sevashramas were very important features of the Ramakrishna Mission medical services, since, whatever aspect the numerous subsequent activities assumed, whether dispensaries, hospitals, polyclinics, they were, as it were, great branching out of the Sevashrama Movement. The organization of a sevashrama is simple enough: the monks dispense medicines or attend to and nurse the patients personally. For the first time, perhaps, in the history of Indian monasticism, sadhus confronted God in pain and suffering in need of the worship of care and ministration. The monks thus openly declared that the invalid, the forlorn, the diseased and the poor were their Gods. Persons lying uncared for by the roadside were the special objects of their adoration. Inspired by the example of Swami Shubhananda and Achalananda, Kalyanananda and Nischayananda, many young workers, monastic and non-monastic, professional doctors and untrained workers came forward to render their honorary service.

The attitude of the workers of the Sevashrama is perhaps best expressed in the words of Swami Nischayananda to 'M', Master Mahashaya. Seeing Swami Nischayananda engaged day and night in work, 'M' remarked: 'Look here Nischay, Thakur used to say, 'The ideal of Sadhu's life is God realization and not mere work.' When 'M' repeated this twice or thrice, Nischayananda could not control himself and bursting into tears said with folded hands, 'I am Swamiji's bond slave; I know no other spiritual practice than work, to which I have been commissioned by him. I have vowed to hold on to this path.' 'M' was not only silenced but understood and apologized. Another monk was engaged in the work of growing vegetables in the fields of Varanasi Sevashrama. When asked why he was thus labouring in the scorching sun when as a monk he should either read Gita or do meditation, he replied unambiguously: 'Why, I am growing vegetables which would be eaten by *Narayana* (the sick).' Yet another monk spent his whole life doing dressings of the wounds of *Rogi-Narayana* (God as sick) to the extent that his knees became stiff due to constant standing. For these monks, work was worship, and the ideal of 'For one's own liberation and for the good of the world' was ever bright before their eyes.

Conclusion

Today the Ramakrishna Mission's medical services range from a humble homoeopathic dispensary to a super-speciality hospital. Yet it does not boast for its numerous medical centers, the large number of patients served, or the high technical sophistication achieved by some of its institutions. Its glory lies in the spirit with which patients are served. One patient served with the right attitude, truly considering him as God, is far superior to serving a multitude without it.

Service of God in Man

*T*he Ramakrishna Mission Home of Service or Sevashrama at Varanasi is now a 230 bedded general hospital with almost all the specialities and even some super specialities, a busy outdoor, a well equipped laboratory, X-Ray and ultra sonography departments, endoscopy and two busy operation theatres. This expansion into a speciality hospital, however, is not the main or spectacular feature of this institution. The dedicated service done in the spirit of worship of God in man by the pioneers and the generation of monks during the early days of the Sevashrama is the most glorious chapter of this institution. It is indeed rewarding and elevating to recapitulate some of those glorious days.

During the early days monks alone took care of the patients. Except for medical consultancy and surgery they did everything pertaining to the care of the patients:

cleaning, sweeping the wards, cleaning the toilets, bed pans and urine pots of the patients, bed making, sponging and cleaning the patients, changing their clothes, implementing the orders of the doctors, administering medicines to the patients, etc. They even assisted the doctors in minor and major operations. They diligently learnt these specialized tasks from the doctors themselves or by some trained male nurse or with the help of books on nursing.

Ban Bihari Maharaj

One of the important tasks was dressing of the wounds, stitching of the cuts and wounds and providing first aid to the injured. Swami Muktananda, endearingly called Ban Bihari Maharaj, did dressings of the patients, considering them as Gods, for more than sixty years. He would reach the dressing room at 8 a.m., put on an apron over his ochre robe and gloves in the hands and would do dressing of the wounds— accidental or surgical—till 2 p.m. or till all the cases were attended. He would again come in the afternoon to boil, wash and dry the linen, bandages, etc. Those were the days when bandages were reused. Ban Bihari Maharaj would do the cleaning, packing and dressing of the wounds as if he were worshipping a God. The result was that the simple dressing room gained an aura of a shrine room. It was indeed a sight for gods to see.

Besides, Ban Bihari Maharaj developed miraculous healing powers. Most difficult and unyielding wounds healed by his touch and even senior surgeons brought their own cases with deep and chronic wounds to him for dressing.

As has already been told, the Sevashrama had started with the treatment of an old lady lying on the roadside. To search for such uncared for poor people, therefore, continued to remain a sacred duty of the monastic workers of the Sevashrama. Such roadside patients were treated with special care, like VIPs. Once the swamis, on their mission of searching such neglected and sick patients—*narayanas*—noticed a mad man with a big wound on his back. They thought this wound, though big, will definitely heal if Ban Bihari Maharaj did the dressings. They therefore brought the mad man, almost by force to the Sevashrama and locked him in a room, so that he may not run away. Ban Bihari Maharaj started doing the dressings and as expected, soon the wound healed.

But although the physical health of the mad man improved, there was no change in his mental condition. What should be done for this? Someone suggested that the patient can be cured if an ayurvedic decoction could be administered to the patient. But a mad patient's cooperation was out of question. The monks, therefore, decided to administer the bitter decoction by force. One person would sit on the chest of the patient and hold his hands on the sides. The other would firmly hold his head steady and forcefully open his mouth and administer the bitter liquid. This technique did work and the patient regained his sanity. He could recollect his whereabouts and was given the rail fare to his home town.

There was another 'Roadside' patient with multiple putrid wounds. Such patients were naturally kept in an isolation ward. Ban Bihari Maharaj started doing dressings of his wounds. But he soon noticed that he

was being neglected by other paid staff—
those responsible for his nursing care. None
liked to go to the patient or to change his
clothes, etc. (This was at a later date when
paid staff had to be employed due to the
lack of monastic workers.) Thus the patient's
general health suffered. Ban Bihari Maharaj
thought of a trick! He called one of the *sevakas*
or servers aside and said, as if confiding
a highly confidential secret: "Look here!
Do you know who this man in the isolation
ward is? He is my father! He has come to
pass his last days in Kashi and final emancipation on leaving his body here. But destiny
has reduced him to such a pitiable state.
However, please do not tell this to anyone,
otherwise. I will be blamed for this—having
become a monk neglecting my father."

This was of course a calculated move
by Ban Bihari Maharaj. The news spread
through gossip and everyone started believ-
ing that the patient was indeed Ban Bihari
Maharaj's father. The result was that he
started getting the best possible care and
food, etc. and rapidly recovered.

Due to standing for long hours
continuously every day for more than sixty

years, Ban Bihari Maharaj's legs had become stiff and in the later years he was not able to bend them. As long as he was able to walk he would go walking to the dressing room from his quarters. When it became difficult, he would go up to the dressing room on a wheel chair and return after doing the dressings standing. A special wheel chair was prepared for him on which he could keep his legs extended while sitting.

A Miracle

While we are recapitulating the stories related to dressings of patients considering them as God, let us narrate an anecdote of another Swami called Ramgati Maharaj. He was an erudite Vedic scholar, who had translated Shankaracharya's commentary on the Brahma Sutras into Bengali with his own comments. He was once posted at the Sevashrama and was engaged in the service of the patients considering them as Gods.

Incidentally, it may be mentioned here that apart from the Belur Math, the three earliest important centres of the Ramakrishna Mission to come up in India were: Advaita

Ashram, Mayavati, Sevashrama at Varanasi and Ramakrishna Math at Madras. These three centres were entirely different from one another. Advaita Ashram was for the study and practice of advaita vedanta bereft of all rituals, forms, etc. Sevashrama at Varanasi was for the practice of service of God in Man and the Math at Madras was devoted to ritualism. All the three are essential for an integrated harmonious spiritual growth. During the early phases of the Ramakrishna Mission, every monk was, as far as possible, posted to all these three centres one after the other so that his spiritual life could flower in a harmonious way. Ramgati Maharaj was no exception. Although a Vedantic scholar, he too was posted at the Sevashrama so that he could put into actual practise the Vedantic dictum "All is Brahman".

Once Swami Saradananda, a direct disciple of Sri Ramakrishna and the then General Secretary of the Ramakrishna Mission, was present at Varanasi Sevashrama, having come there on an official visit. One day Ramgati Maharaj approached him with a problem. Although whole heartedly willing to serve the patients in a spirit of worship considering them as Gods, at times he was not even able to approach them due to very foul and putrid smell of the wounds to be dressed. Just then, there was a patient with gangrenous wound and the Swami found it extremely hard even to approach him due to very foul smell.

Swami Saradananda heard the complaint and became serious. He then told the young Swami to pray to Sri Ramakrishna for help. And a miracle happened. Next day the Swami did not get the stink at all and since then he was able to approach and dress the patients without any difficulty!

Silent Sweepers

For these dedicated monks, there was no work too lowly or menial. They even competed with each other in doing menial works like sweeping and cleaning the latrines. There are two interesting stories depicting this.

One morning, when the monk assigned the duty of cleaning the latrines, bedpans, etc. reached the ward, he found that everything had been cleaned. Since all the patients were sleeping, none could say who had done it. This happened for a few days subsequently. Finally, to investigate the matter, the monk one day reached the spot much before schedule and hid himself. Finally he found the Secretary of the Sevashrama himself walking in and washing the place. When "caught red-handed" the Secretary Swami said he did so for he too wanted to render some service. Had he come during day time, he would not have been allowed to do so. At this the junior monk said that just as he is serving by cleaning the place and utensils, the Secretary was also doing service sitting in his office.

It is said that in a similar case, it was noticed that one unknown person would come from outside and quietly go away after cleaning the place and dirty utensils. When the monks tried to catch him, he dodged them and never came again. His identity ever remained unknown.

Patient Turned Nurse

Such dedicated service naturally was infectious. Many lay people got impressed and joined the monks in this great sacrifice of dedicated service of Living Gods. But the most inspiring and touching case is that of a patient who was so inspired that on being cured, offered his services for the service of the sick gods. And it so happened that this patient turned nurse had to nurse a patient of small pox. He did it with utmost dedication. Finally the patient of small pox survived and recovered but the patient turned nurse contracted small pox and finally died of it uttering the name of Sri Ramakrishna. Swami Shivananda, Mahapurush Maharaj, was so overwhelmed by this incident that he wrote a special article in the Udbodhan as a tribute to this noble sacrifice.

Work is Worship

The activities of the Sevashrama were based upon the sacred principle that all creatures are divine and that the service of man is service to God, as taught by Sri Ramakrishna: "*Shiva Jnane Jiva Seva*".

Swami Vivekananda too had asserted this over and over again in his teachings. Hence when in 1902 Swami Vivekananda had visited Varanasi for the last time, he was very happy to see the activities of the young group of devotees who had started the Sevashrama in a rented house. He therefore instructed Swami Brahmananda to encourage the workers later also. Since this time, stalwarts like Swami Brahmananda and Swami Turiyananda and later Swami Atmananda and Swami Achalananda constantly laboured to provide spiritual direction to the apparently secular services. Whenever Swami Brahmananda was present at the Sevashrama, he emphasized that spiritual practices like Japa and meditation must be done regularly by every worker. He would personally inquire into the spiritual welfare of each worker and give specific spiritual guidance.

Later Swami Turiyananda lived for many years at Varanasi Sevashrama and through talks and discussions always kept the minds of the workers at a high spiritual level. After Turiyanandaji passed away, Swami Atmananda, an austere contemplative disciple of Swami Vivekananda was sent to Varanasi Sevashrama so that he may inspire the workers to lead a God-centred life. Work cannot be converted into worship without simultaneously doing conventional spiritual practices like Japa, meditation, study of scriptures, etc.

For example, we are liable to forget that the human being is an image of God. And repeated reminders are required. Swami Achalananda, one of the disciples of Swami Vivekananda and later one of the Vice-Presidents of the Ramakrishna Mission, lived for many years at Varanasi Sevashrama. He would not even speak the word 'patient'. Instead he would always ask, "How many Narayanas have been admitted today? How many Narayanas have been discharged?" He would be annoyed if anyone used the word 'patient'. The whole setup of the Sevashrama is like that of a temple. There is no separate temple or shrine other than the buildings in which patients *Narayanas* are housed. The kitchen where food for the sick *narayanas* is cooked is called "*Narayana Bhandar*". Food is first served to the "*Narayanas*" around 10 a.m. Later the same food is served to the workers, both lay and monastic, the idea being that the food has become consecrated by being offered to sick-*narayanas* first.

The financial condition of the Sevashrama was never very good. But by the grace of the Divine Mother, there was never any dearth of bare subsistence. The services offered were completely free of charge and the institution depended totally on charity. It was natural that at times there was acute financial crisis. During such periods, the workers, both monastic and lay, would assemble together for introspection to find out why such a crisis has occurred. For they had the firm faith that if their service was truly unselfish and done in the spirit of real worship, there won't be any financial difficulty. After personal and collective heart searching when they rectified their defects, it was found that money started flowing in automatically. There was a time during the earlier periods when the workers served the sick-narayanas in the morning and later got their food by begging. It was almost compulsory for all monks to attend "Sadhu Bhandaras", feasts for Sadhus, in which they were invited outside the Sevashrama, for that meant so much saving of food at the Sevashrama!

This task of service of God in man has to be done not only by the monastic members of the Ramakrishna Order who have dedicated themselves to the fulfillment of Swami Vivekananda's mission, but by all the devotees and admirers of Swamiji. Let this ideal of service to God in man penetrate so deep, spread so wide and extend so long into society that it may become part and parcel of the culture and thought-life of society. All those who engage in such service of the poor, the destitute or otherwise needy in one way or the other, are indeed blessed.

Spiritually Tackling Problems of Old Age

*A*lthough old age forms an integral phase in the life of all creatures, Geriatrics—the branch of medicine dealing with problems of old age—is only of recent origin. Till a few decades ago, medical problems of old age did not form a part of the curriculum of medical studies. This emphasis on the problems of ageing seems to be the result partly of the trend towards specialization and super-specialization and partly of certain sociological changes like phenomenal increase in nuclear families all over the world. In traditional joint families, senior citizens lived with their children and grand-children and were affectionately looked after, and in their turn they played specific role in rearing up the grand-children and transmitting family traditions to the posterity. All this has now changed. The senior citizens today feel neglected, helpless and unwanted, and senior citizens' homes are increasing everywhere.

While these might have been the recent trends, the specific psychological and physiological problems of ageing are the same from time immemorial. In old age, the human metabolism changes–it becomes more catabolic than anabolic; major hormonal changes occur causing specific mental and physical effects, and degenerative process overtakes almost every organ of the body. A senior citizen might still resemble a youth in form and figure, but in many respects he belongs to a different class or biological species, as it were. Geriatric physiology is different from infantile physiology and bio-chemistry. Geriatric pathology and disease patterns are much different from those of childhood and youth. Nay, even the pharmacology, surgery and medicine of the elderly are specific. It is no wonder, then, that Geriatrics as a specialized branch of medicine should rapidly evolve, with release of scores of books and a few journals on Geriatrics in recent times.

While modern medical science might have been late in recognizing the problems of aging and tackling them, all ancient spiritual traditions of the world had recognized ageing as a phase to be dealt with in a specific way. Hinduism had divided the span of human life into four ashramas: *brahmacharya, garhasthya, vanaprastha and sannyasa.* After fulfilling one's duties as a householder in the second stage of life, the *garhasthya,* the individual was supposed to retire and devote more and more to the worship of God, study, contemplation and self control as a *vanaprasthin,* till he or she was ready to embrace the life of a recluse or *sannyasin,* characterised by total renunciation. This custom had got so ingrained in the cultural pattern of the Hindus that many would retire to holy places like Kashi, Vrindaban, etc. to spend their last days there in some ashramas in religious practices. Although now senior citizens' homes have come up at these pilgrim spots, one can still find a number of dharmashalas and homes of the ancient type for retired people, with good or indifferent living facilities.

Spiritual literature of all religions is also replete with references to old age and death–the two unwelcome but inevitable eventualities. It is true, however, that death had scared humans more than old age. Man had, from ancient times, tried more to prolong his life, to become immortal, to know the secret of death, than to remain young. Such is the intense clinging to life that an old man with multiple infirmities, disabilities, and severe pain does not want to die. Nachiketa had enquired about the secret of death from Yama, the king of death. Maitreyi, the wife of Yajnavalkya, the sage of the Brihadaranyaka, wanted to know from her husband the way by which she could become immortal.

We also get warnings about the suffering staring at humans in the form of old age. One of the three painful sights which prince Gautama, the future Buddha, saw was an old man. The Bhagavad Gita advises us to contemplate upon the suffering ingrained in birth, death, old age and disease. In the Episode of Puranjana in the fourth skandha of Srimad Bhagavatam, old age is depicted as an ugly grey haired unwanted daughter of Time, and the sister of *bhaya*, fear.

That a youth lived recklessly in uncontrolled sense enjoyments leads to a miserable old age is often depicted in religious stories, hymns and songs. King Yayati led a life of sense indulgence. When his youth was abruptly terminated due to a curse, he felt extremely miserable, because his mind was full of unquenched desires which he was not able to satisfy due to the decayed senses of enjoyment. Sri Shankaracharya describes such a wretched plight thus:

'Limbs have become weak and infirm, head is covered with grey hair, mouth has lost all teeth, and the old man totters with a stick, yet, alas, desire for sense-enjoyment does not leave him.'

The *Bhajagovindam* stotra again refers to old age as a state characterized by innumerable anxieties. Another poet very graphically describes old age thus: 'When the body becomes old, the person goes on worrying about wealth and people consider him crazy.' And according to another, 'When a person becomes old, *kapha* and *vayu* attack him—he becomes subject to a number of diseases and remains lying on the cot day and night.' In all these popular songs the exhortation is to devote oneself to religious and spiritual practices and to start contemplation of God even while young.

This we can clearly see in the lives of the saints. Most of the great spiritual acharyas and prophets led an intense spiritual life from the beginning. Sri Shankaracharya died at the age of thirty two and Jesus Christ at thirty three. Swami Vivekananda stood as the world teacher on the platform of the Parliament of Religions when he was just thirty years old. Saint Francis lived only for forty four years and Sri Ramakrishna only fifty. These great spiritual giants did not wait for their body growing old. And yet, they were far more wise and mature than many old men and women.

In spiritual traditions maturity is given far greater importance than ageing. Indeed seniority can be of three different types. A person older in age is called a senior citizen-*vaya-jyeshtha*. There is another seniority—professional seniority—*paryaya jyeshtha*. A person may be young in age, but if he or she has joined certain services at a younger age, he or she might rise to a higher hierarchical position than his colleagues elder to him in age. Finally there is a third type of seniority: *jnana-jyeshtha*—seniority with regard to wisdom. A person may be young in age, even junior in professional cadre, but may be wiser, more learned and mature. Referring to this last type of maturity, it is said in the *Dakshinamurti stotra*:

'Under a banyan tree elderly disciples are sitting surrounding a young guru. Guru is dispelling the doubts of the disciples by his silent sermon. Oh! What a wonderful sight it was!'

No better example of this can be found than that of Shukadeva, a teenaged boy expounding the Bhagavatam to the venerable sages many times elder to him. Although worldly people may grow physically old, they remain mentally and spiritually immature, while a spiritual person might remain physically young, but may have grown mature intellectually and spiritually.

It may also be mentioned that ageing, to a large extent, is dependent upon the mental attitude of the individual. We often speak of people who are enthusiastic, enterprising and optimistic as eighty years 'young'. In contrast, there could be lifeless, depressed men and women in their thirties or forties who lose all their zeal and vigour. They are no better than the old. It is therefore but natural that in all spiritual traditions much greater stress is laid on intellectual, ethical and spiritual maturity, and the disciplines required to attain it, than on the problems of physical aging.

And yet, the fact is that only the old people, after wasting or enjoying their youth, turn towards spiritual life in their old age—more out of frustration and necessity, rather than real interest in spirituality. There is a popular notion that one should enjoy life as long as one is young and should turn to religious or spiritual life only in the old age; spiritual life is for the elderly and not for the young. There is an interesting joke. One old man said to his young son, 'My dear son, I want to tell you about a warning I received from my father, which unfortunately I did not heed to. When I was young, my father told me not to lead a reckless life, but to lead a constrained regulated life, otherwise I would suffer in old age. I did not listen to his advice and indeed, I am suffering. So I want to warn you to devote yourself to a life of contemplation and self–restraint from now on, otherwise, you too will suffer like me.' The son reverently listened to his father and respectfully replied, 'Yes, father, what you say is true. When I shall grow old, I too shall convey this warning to my son!'

Nothing could be more fallacious than this notion that religion is something to be practised in old age. Unless a person gets used to contemplation at a younger age, he or she can never devote himself or herself to God in old age. Impressions of a worldly or sensuous life led in youth don't fade easily and an old man is likely to face greater failures and frustrations if he begins a religious life too late.

Once Swami Saradananda gave a very salutary advise to Swami Nikhilananda, when the latter had approached him as a young man:

'It is good to be active, but it depends on several factors. Your health must be good. ... But suppose you have injured one of your limbs, then it would be difficult for you to work. Therefore I request you to cultivate the habit of reading. Even that is not enough. Suppose you become blind. Therefore it is good that you practise meditation so that if you cannot read or work, at least you can meditate.'[1]

To be able to benefit by spirituality in the old age, therefore, it is important that we train ourselves spiritually years before we grow old. Let us, while still young, observe the plight of the elderly and realize that one day we too might have to face the same fate of disease and disability, of despair and neglect. Let us prepare ourselves mentally and spiritually from now on without wasting a single moment.

While this is the general rule, there is no cause for total despair for those who have already neglected their precious youthful years. It is never too late and one can begin at any age. The celebrated Christian saint, Brother Lawrence, had once written to a woman in the world who was past sixty:

'Begin then; perhaps He is waiting for a single generous resolution. Have courage. There is but little time to live; you are nearly

---

1. Swami Asheshananda, *Glimpses of a Great Soul,* Vedanta Press, Hollywood, 1982, p.243.

sixty four and I am almost eighty. Let us live and die with God. ....'[1]

There are innumerable examples of saints who had wasted their youth in frivolous pursuits, but when at an advanced age they turned to spiritual life, they quickly rose to great spiritual heights due to their sincere and intense spiritual effort. Girish Chandra Ghosh, the renowned dramatist-playwright of Bengal is one such saint. Swami Advaitananda, a monastic disciple of Sri Ramakrishna, was fifty-five years old–even older than his guru, Sri Ramakrishna–when he first came in contact with the latter. Much, therefore, depends upon one's urge for spirituality.

One of the cardinal values which can help the senior citizens is 'faith'. Faith, either in a superhuman controlling power or in one's own higher self, has tremendous integrating and stabilizing power. While we are discussing the effectivity of faith, we may also try to realize what is meant by the word spirituality. Just as by 'materialism' is meant

---

1. Brother Lawrence, *Practice of the Presence of God*, St.Paul Publication, Mumbai, 1997.

the view that matter is the only reality and the pursuit of material or mundane goals the only true purpose of life, similarly by spirituality is meant the view that the non-material spirit or soul or atman is the only reality and the true nature of man. Such a view advocates pursuit of a spiritual goal in life. The Sanskrit word for 'spiritual' is *adhyatmic*–which is significant. It means that which concerns the self, the individual. Thus spiritual approach to problems, personal or collective, is essentially oriented towards the individual. A spiritual person believes in changing himself or herself rather than others. Our problems are caused not merely by external influences but also by the way we react to them. We don't have much control on external factors, but we can change ourselves. Spiritual approach teaches us to take the responsibility on ourselves and not blame others.

Many of the religious and spiritual practices prevalent in various world religions can definitely help in solving at least some of the problems of old age. The physical problems of ageing fall under the purview of Medicine but the psychological and social problems of senior citizens can, to a large extent, be tackled with the help of spirituality.

Rituals form an important part of all spiritual traditions. They are, in fact, spiritual truths concretized and expressed in gross forms and acts. These ritual exercises are easy to practise and provide sanctifying occupation to the individual. Senior citizens find delight in cleaning the shrine room, decorating the images and pictures of gods and goddesses with flowers, preparing garlands and such other little acts associated with a chapel or a shrine or a religious place, private or public. Senior citizens' homes in the vicinity of such religious places have this added advantage that they provide scores of such opportunities for their inmates. If there is no such centre of spiritual activity, a small shrine or chapel can be made in one's home or in the senior citizens' homes.

Study of scriptures or spiritual literature or listening to such discourses is also a very effective technique to drive away melancholy and elevate the mood of the senior citizens. Religious TV serials on national channels or on special TV channels specializing in them serve the same purpose. Audio and video cassettes of spiritual programmes is a gift of modern technology which can be made use of with advantage. Devotional songs act as excellent occupation to the senior citizens. Many senior citizens engage themselves in doing Japa and meditation. While meditation may be difficult, Japa can certainly be done. Following a spiritual routine gives a great sense of well-being.

Conclusion

Although it is wise to be fore-warned about the problems of old age, there is nothing to be afraid of therein. It is inevitable and one must face it with courage. Medical science can help in tackling the physical problems of aging. Religion and spirituality can greatly help in the psychological and social rehabilitation of the senior citizens. Above all, spirituality provides a healthy attitude, a sane philosophy and stabilizing faith in the fragile depressive period of old age. Spirituality must be incorporated in any programme for the care of the elderly.

The Nobility of the Medical Profession

*O*f the various professions, I consider three as the noblest: the medical, the teachers' and of a spiritual instructor, guide, guru or monk. For, these three make the three gifts: of health or *arogya dana*, of learning or *vidya dana* and of spiritual knowledge or *jnana dana*. Traditionally these three gifts were made free, and were called *dana*, and the giver was given in exchange whatever the receiver considered suitable as *dakshina*. And even till a few decades ago, this noble custom had continued in India. It is only recently that due to the impact of western civilization and commercialization of all aspects of life that these have been converted into bread-winning professions.

The health care professionals are the most fortunate and the most privileged class of people in the society. For, they have got an opportunity to learn and practice the most prestigious, most responsible and the noblest profession. The nobility of the medical profession–in any form, as doctors, technicians, nursing staff–cannot be over-emphasized. Unfortunately, not many really appreciate its nobility. They realize that it is a very lucrative profession and they can gain name, fame and prestige by it. It opens up a number of opportunities for worldly success. But not many realize that the medical profession also opens wide the door for higher pursuits, higher than merely name and fame.

While engaged in their professional activities, being busy with the technical and academic pursuits of their professional science, the doctors and para–medical people are at times apt to lose sight of the ethical, human, psychological and spiritual aspects of their profession. This is all the more true in the modern times which can be termed as a period of technicalization, specialization and commercialization. These developments have seriously hampered the doctor-patient relationship, which, only a few decades ago was very healthy and fulfilling. Today, medical profession has come under the purview of the 'Consumer Protection Act'. Indeed, medical activity has now become a business, a contract, made and executed on financial basis, rather than an act of worship, as Swami Vivekananda had envisaged.

Some of the medical personnel may not be inclined to bring in God into their profession. For them—indeed for all—let me quote a passage from the *Introduction* of the First Edition of the *Harrison's Text-book of Medicine* which emphasizes the glory and dignity of the medical profession in a forceful manner:

'No greater opportunity, obligation or responsibility can fall to the lot of a human being than to become a physician (or a doctor). In the care of the sick he/she needs technical skill, scientific knowledge and human understanding. He/she who uses these with wisdom, with courage and with humility will render a unique service to his/her fellow beings and would build within himself or herself, an enduring edifice of character. A physician must seek for his/

her destiny no more than these. He/she must be content with no less.

The Aims of Medical Profession: Service and Character

The author has the boldness to state plainly that the aims, the goals, of the medical profession are only two: service and building one's character; not money, name or fame, prestige or position. These will come. Swami Vivekananda says: 'In the world take always the position of the giver. Give everything and look for no return. Give love, give help, give service, give any little thing you can, but keep out barter. Make no conditions, and none will be imposed. Let us give out of our own bounty, just as God gives to us.'[1] Unfortunately in our short sightedness, we forget this. 'Unselfishness is more paying but people don't have the patience to practice it.'[2]

The author says that the medical profession provides the greatest opportunity. Why? Does not a monk of the Ramakrishna

1. CW VII, p.5.
2. CW I, p.32.

Mission, for example, get greater opportunity for service and character building? No. The medical profession has much greater opportunity. He can serve the patients as God. By considering the patients as God, he will be able to convert his work into the highest spiritual practice—a means of liberation or *moksha*. Thus medical profession not only gives an opportunity to serve, but can also lead to the highest spiritual goal of life: *moksha*. It is conductive to all the four *purusharthas*: *dharma*, *artha*, *kama* and *moksha*.

Apart from service to one's fellow beings, the author of this article suggests another aim and achievement on which a medical professional must have his eye. And that is character. Swami Vivekananda says, 'Money does not pay, nor name; fame does not pay, nor learning. It is love that pays; it is character that cleaves through the adamantine walls of difficulties.'[1] We know the other sayings: 'If you are planning for a year, sow a crop. If you are planning for 10 years or 25 years, plant a tree. But if you

---

1. CW IV, p.367.

are planning for a hundred years, build character.' And another: 'If money is lost, nothing is lost; if health is lost, something is lost; but if character is lost, everything is lost.' Our greatest contribution, our role for society would be to build a noble character, apart from service. But character is not formed in a day. It takes years of persistent, continuous and uninterrupted, diligent effort. The medical professionals have greatest opportunity for this.

Responsibility and Obligation

Now, I come to the word used in the first line in the quotation: *responsibility*. No greater responsibility could fall to a human being's lot. Yes, today the responsibility of the medical professionals is the greatest. It goes on increasing as they become senior, as they mature. They have a responsibility towards their families, the society, the nation in the larger sense and towards their juniors, students, colleagues and patients, in the limited sense. Above all, they have the greatest responsibility towards the profession, and towards the prestigious, noble institutions from where they have graduated or where they have received the best possible training.

Medical professionals have also got the greatest obligation. For what? Again, to serve. They are responsible to the society, to the nation, for their deeds and professional behaviour. A soldier in war has to be very careful, his officer has to be still more careful not to take a wrong decision. For, the life of so many soldiers depends on it. Similarly, one wrong decision of a medical man–a physician, surgeon or a technician–can lead to the death of a patient.

There was a time when a doctor was worshipped. Today, he is seen with suspicion. The younger generation has no role models. They see the unethical doctors flourishing. The ethical degradation of the profession is appalling, and it is the responsibility of the doctors that by their noble ethical conduct, they re-establish its noble image in the minds of the public and set a equally noble example before the younger generation.

In modern times there has occurred a steady commercialization of the medical profession. An ethically decadent society cannot last long. It is the responsibility of each person to keep up high ethical standard. In the present age of globalization each individual is as important as anyone else. One vote can topple a government. The instability of Indian government has repercussions on American economy. What we think and how we act affects the whole world. This must be deeply understood. Let us not think that if we act unethically, it will not matter to the society. Let us begin the process of ethical revival from now on.

Hence the role of medical professionals in the society is twofold: taking care of society's physical health and second, taking care of its ethical health.

Technical Skill and Scientific Knowledge

In the care of the sick the medical man or woman needs these two: technical skills and scientific knowledge. Some may learn technical skill but may lack theoretical knowledge. This is dangerous. This is quackery. Both are needed. Mere theoretical knowledge is not enough. The medical teaching institutions teach both. Both must be made use of. It is extremely important to upgrade the knowledge and skill through reading literature and by refresher courses, etc.

Human Understanding

While we have scientific knowledge and technical skill, the author has also mentioned *human understanding*. This is something which one may not learn in a medical institute, but may have to learn by personal experience or from the example of the seniors. This is a very important quality. Doctors must be very careful not to reduce themselves into medical technicians who only mend a human machine which has become defective. Man is not merely a biological unit made up of certain cells and organs, but he has also a psychology. He is a social and psychological unit. Disease is a tremendous stress on him, mentally, economically and socially. A doctor must have this understanding of the other dimensions of the patient's personality. One person falling ill disturbs not only him, but his family, his office, and many more units of which he is a part.

You need human understanding– nay, humane understanding, to grasp these deeper dimensions of illness. I would recommend that all read the third chapter of the first edition of *Oxford Textbook of Medicine* entitled *Medicine in an Unjust World*, by M.H. King, who has also written a book on how to develop a clinical laboratory in a developing country with minimal financial resources. This article will introduce medical men to socio-economics of medicine. It will give them a wider vision of the medical world, will help them decide the strategy of medical planning. Do we want more super–specialities for few rich people or do we want basic primary health care, maternal and child health care for the larger population? These questions are discussed by Dr. King. This article was considered so important–and indeed it is of prime importance–that it was thought fit to be included in the beginning of so important a text book of medicine.

If you have human understanding you will not only decide to serve the poor, the less privileged in society, but your approach towards each individual will also be one of sympathy and deep understanding. You will win friends as well.

Wisdom and Courage

It is very important to use the knowledge and skill we have with wisdom. Wisdom means the ability to discriminate between what is right and what is wrong, what is harmful and what is beneficial, what is moral and what is immoral. Sometimes we might be confused. Hence wisdom must be painstakingly cultivated. If we use the knowledge and skill for selfish purposes, for exploiting the patient who comes to us in a helpless condition, if we use them unethically, we are not using wisdom, we are not being wise. This is an unwise use of science and technology. And this, unfortunately, has become the modern trend. With all the scientific knowledge, we have not been able to build a peaceful, humanitarian society. We have built up an exploitative society. It is the prime duty of the medical professionals not to misuse in any way their skill and knowledge.

Then, the medical professionals also need courage—courage to take bold decisions and equally bold action. To be able to take courageous, wise decision and act accordingly, with a cool, collected mind, by carefully evaluating the pros and cons of a particular action, is the quality of a highly cultured mind and the medical profession offers one of the greatest and rarest opportunities for this. As a medical professional attempts such bold decisions, in due course his power of judgement also improves.

Humility

Finally, the author of the article asks the doctors to have one rare quality: humility, lack of vanity, pride and arrogance. A conscientious medical professional is bound to gradually become humble. No other profession than the medical shows us greater miracles of God. Those who have long years of medical experience would testify how many times their judgements have failed. There are cases which the doctors consider, from the medical point of view, hopeless, with no chance of recovery or survival, but they survive. And are there not scores of cases which the doctors thought are doing well, suddenly deteriorate and succumb? A conscientious doctor, with faith in God cannot but realize that he is merely an instrument in the hands of a far greater power and intelligence who is moving him at will like a puppet.

Sri Ramakrishna says that God laughs twice: Once when two brothers divide a piece of land by a line telling this much is mine, that one yours. God laughs to think that after all the land belongs to me. Second time God laughs when a doctor assures the mother of a sick child that he will save it. The doctor forgets that life and death are in the hands of God.

Let the doctors therefore humble themselves so that they may become fit instruments in the hands of God. Let them begin their professional day with a prayer to God that He may make them his fit instruments.

Humility is a sublime virtue. It adds to the lusture, as it were, of the noble character of a knowing and efficient medical professional.

Medical Profession, a Worship

The medical profession can also be practised in the spirit of worship of God. Let me explain to you what I mean by medical profession being a worship. Swami

Vivekananda, while establishing the Rama-krishna Mission a century ago, gave it a motto: 'Shiv Jnane Jiva Seva': service of the human being considering him or her Shiva or God. And he also showed how to do it. He said, 'You have read: "Look upon your mother as God, look upon your father as God". But I say, the poor, the illiterate, the ignorant, the afflicted, let these be your God.'[1] In the Ramakrishna Mission, the monastic members as well as the lay devotees try to put this into actual practice.

At the Ramakrishna Mission's 230 bedded hospital at Varanasi the monks serve the patients considering them as gods. There is no temple. The hospital itself is the temple. The hospital kitchen where patients' food is cooked is called 'Narayan Bhandar' i.e. the Kitchen of the Lord. At around 10 o'clock, food is served to the Rogi-Narayana, patient-gods, and the same food the monks eat around 12 o'clock. That means, the food, having been first offered to Narayana, has now become a sacrament, *prasad*, which the monks, the worshippers, partake with reverence.

---

1. CW VI, p.288.

Just as in a temple we worship Shiva–
as Shivalingam or Laxmi or Venkateswara,
with lighted lamp, food offerings, incense,
flowers etc., similar worship can be done
of a Sick Narayana. Of course, we don't
offer these items. Instead of water to bathe
the deity, we sponge the patient-Narayana
with medicated lotion. Instead of flowers
we offer eye drops or tablets; instead of
sandal paste, we dress the wounds and
apply ointment. And instead of chanting
mantras in Sanskrit, we tell words of consolation and encouragement to our patient–
God. Thus, our act of examining and
treating a patient gets transformed into a
worship. And indeed, how closely does an
elaborate surgical operation resemble a
special puja like Durga or Vinayaka Puja
during the special days! The operation
theatre can be compared to the Puja
Mandapam, where the surgeon is the chief
priest; the anesthetist, the chief attendant
or the Tantra dharaka and the many assistants are like so many assistants in a worship.
And is it not a fact that the surgical opera-
tion-worship is also conducted with equal
gravity and solemnity?

This is the spirit with which monks served and are still serving patients at the Ramakrishna Mission's medical institutions. For them, the medical service is neither a profession nor even a service, but a spiritual practice, sadhana, comparable to meditation which would lead them to God or moksha. And every doctor can and must sublimate his medical activity into a spiritual act. What is required is a change in one's attitude. Let them begin the day with reminding themselves that the patients they are going to meet are veritable embodiments of God, and let them try to act accordingly.

Spiritual Phenomenon in the Light of Bio-Technology

Introduction

If we trace the evolution of the inter-action between modern science and religion, we shall find that at one time, may be upto two centuries ago, modern science was in its infancy and there was no organized branch called holistic science. Instead, there was religion—although a science in itself—based mainly on faith, only vaguely understood. Even this faith had a rational and experiential basis, which was not well understood. During this phase religion vehemently opposed modern science. Galileo was humiliated and Bruno was burnt alive.

But modern science maintained its relentless march and soon religion was on the defensive. Modern scientific discoveries shattered faith in heaven and hell, even disproved God. It was during this period of scientific ascendancy that Swami Vivekananda presented to the West Vedanta as the scientific religion.

We are now in the third phase when modern science, having realized its theoretical as well as applied limitations, and having appreciated the scientific nature of religion and its usefulness for the individual and society, has decided not only to shake hands with it—now called holistic science—but also try to understand it with its own tools of investigation.

The first to change stance was physics—atomic physics, or more precisely, sub-atomic and quantum physics. Its discoveries were so startling that we heard great modern physicists speak like mystics, and people started telling that religion and science are shaking hands. But physics is only one branch of modern science. Biology, physiology, and medical science are also material sciences. Even psychology is a science—science of the psyche or mind. And, it did not take long for honest modern scientists to realize that mysticism is also a science—science of the spirit. But there are other scientists also, who are not willing to assign the term 'science' to mysticism. Instead, they try to understand mysticism and spiritual phenomenon with the help of modern scientific methods, which they feel are the only authentic tools to understand everything happening in the world, internal or external.

Spiritual Phenomenon

Before we take up the study of spiritual experience in the light of modern science, especially neuro-sciences, we must clearly understand what spirituality means. Swami Vivekananda equates religion with realization: "If there is God, we must see Him; if there is a soul, we must realize it." So, then, religion is not merely faith, but realization——a real, mystic experience. But that is not all. Religion is also 'being and becoming', and a transformation of personality.

But how are spiritual experience and transformation related, if at all? The great spiritual masters tell us that true spiritual experience cannot be obtained unless one passes through rigorous and prolonged spiritual discipline for many many years. Without such a discipline, if the person obtains an experience, it will either be misunderstood or will not last long. Cases are on record of such "stumbling upon truth" without due preparation, and the result of such an experience had been beneficial as well as harmful to the individual and society.

Secondly, a genuine spiritual experience must transform the personality of the experiencer. Swami Vivekananda has categorically said that if a fool enters samadhi (super-conscious experience) he comes out a saint. The real spiritual experience is so profound that it wholly transforms the character of the individual. And this aspect of religion is far more important than experience. Take for example the three descriptions of ideal states to be attained in the Bhagavad Gita: the *sthitaprajna*, the ideal bhakta, and the *trigunatita*. Although there is no mention of spiritual experience there, a detailed description of the moral and ethical characteristics of a person are described. Here is the description of an ideal bhakta, paraphrased by Swami Vivekananda:

"'He who hates none, who is the friend of all, who is merciful to all, who has nothing of his own, who is free from egoism, who is even-minded in pain and pleasure, who is forbearing, who is always satisfied, who works always in Yoga, whose self has become controlled, whose will is firm, whose mind and intellect are given up unto Me, such a one is My beloved Bhakta. From whom comes no disturbance, who cannot be disturbed by others, who is pure and active, who does not care whether good comes or evil, and never becomes miserable, who has given up all efforts for himself; who is the same in praise or in blame, with a silent, thoughtful mind, blessed with what little comes in his way, homeless, for the whole world is his home, and who is steady in his ideas, such a one is My beloved Bhakta.' Such alone become Yogis."[1]

In Sri Ramakrishna we see a complete demonstration of the spiritual phenomenon. He often used to have samadhi and varied

1. *Complete Works*, Vol. 1, page 193.

spiritual experiences. With this, he was wholly established in moral values like truth, unselfishness, renunciation, continence, non-possessiveness, purity, love and compassion, etc. This was not all. Even his nervous system had been transformed. He could not touch a coin, even in sleep; and would feel pain if his hand touched a woman. He would feel lost if he unconsciously or unknowingly possessed even a little packet of condiments! In short, we find all the three features of spiritual phenomenon—experience, moral excellence and physiological transformation—in Sri Ramakrishna.[1]

With this short introduction about what spiritual phenomenon actually is, let us now turn to psycho-neurology.

Psycho-Neurology

This branch of physiology identifies the areas of nervous system associated with spiritual phenomenon and mental

---

1. For details of Sri Ramakrishna's physiology, please consult *"Physiology of a Man of God"* by Dr. C.S. Shah, *The Vedanta Kesari*, May, June and August 1999.

modifications, thoughts, emotions, instincts, etc. Recently a new discipline called Neuro-theology has come up. It studies the neuro-biology of spirituality and religion. Its aim is to identify regions of the brain which are associated with spiritual experiences, especially the sense of the presence of God or God realization.

Andrew Newberg and Eugene D'Aquilli used a brain-imaging technique called Single Photon Emission Computed Tomography (SPECT) to determine regions of brain which respond to altered states of consciousness during prayer and meditation. The experiments were carried out on Tibetan Buddhists and Franciscan nuns. They recorded an increased activity in the frontal lobe area of brain—it "lights up" at the peak of meditation. They also found that there is reduction of activity in parietal lobe of brain. Parietal lobe is also known as Oriental Association Area (OAA) since it controls our sense of space. It requires continuous sensory inputs to do its job. During intense meditation, no activity was observed in OAA. During transcendental spiritual experience, OAA is dormant and boundaries between self and other worldly things are dissolved. A state of absolute calmness and contentment is attained—self appears united with God. The temporal lobes help to relate religious symbols or images to feelings, thus triggering a sense of awe. When the temporal lobes are artificially stimulated, a sense of divine presence is felt.[1]

Using an ordinary motorcycle helmet, modified with electro-magnetic coils, Dr. Persinger was able to artificially induce a profound spiritual experience. This device works by inducing very small electrical signals with tiny magnetically induced mechanical vibrations, in the brain cells of temporal lobes and other selected areas of the brain. These lobes produce what are called "Forty Hertz Component" of brain waves detected in electro encephalogram. These "FHC" are present during waking and dream state, but are absent during deep sleep. These FHCs are important for the experience of the personal self or reality. By suppressing the FHCs the sense of individual self is reduced. This is what

---

1. *Divine Experience and Neurobiology*, by P.N. Jha, Times of India, Thursday, July 4, 2002.

Dr. Persinger's helmet does. When brain is deprived of self-stimulation and sensory input required for defining itself as being distinct from the world, the brain 'defaults' to a sense of infinity. So the experience of self simply expands to fill the perception of the world. One experiences becoming one with the world.[1]

Neuro-scientists have given another interesting explanation for "God realization." There are two temporal lobes in the brain: the right and the left, which are connected to each other. Sometimes this connection gets disturbed by sickness, stress and strain, the FH components also get disorganized and then the normally silent right hand sense of self is experienced by the left hand sense of self. The scientists call this God experience an experience of another self within the self!!

The electro-magnetic helmet experiment is interesting. Although the experiment is described, we don't have the follow up to show whether there was any change in the character and conduct of those who were subjected to it. It must be emphasized that in spiritual traditions, such 'God experiences',

---

1. http://www.bidstrup.com/mystic.htm.

or experience of unity, etc. are not granted to disciples without years of arduous practice of spiritual discipline, for two reasons:

1. Without due preparation, they would not be able to retain and keep it up, and,

2. More importantly, such 'God experiences' granted or obtained without proper purification can have dangerous repercussions for the individual or society. It is on record that such "stumbling upon truth" has resulted in bringing out the angel as well as the devil out of the person.

Another point to remember, therefore, is that spiritual life is not merely an isolated experience—it is a phenomenon, which includes transformation of character and conduct as well as rigorous spiritual practice. In the long run, the spiritual phenomenon leads even to total change in the nervous system, to the extent of changing the psychic and physiological reflex actions, as had happened in Sri Ramakrishna.

Psycho-Surgery

Psycho-surgery is the scientific method of treatment of mental disorders by means of brain surgery. Although such a surgery was performed in 1894 by a Swiss doctor, this operation of destruction of the frontal lobes of brain for treatment of emotional disorders was technically advanced by Sir Victor Horsley in UK and Harvey Cushing in USA. Later in 1931, operation called lobotomy, or leucotomy was developed, which consisted to severing nerve-fibre tracts between the thalamus and frontal lobes by using a special knife called leucotome. Later a quick and easy procedure called "Trans orbital leucotomy" was developed which could be done within few minutes under local anaesthesia. Thus in 40's and 50's more than 50,000 persons were subjected to lobotomy all over the world, based on very scanty and flimsy (and even unwarranted) evidence for its scientific basis. Soon it became evident that although lobotomy was able to control severely agitated and violent behaviour and becalm psychotic patients, there were many undesirable side effects. Pre-frontal lobotomy produced "zombies"—persons without emotions, apathetic to everything and with reduced drive and having no initiative. They also lost several important higher mental functions such as socially adequate behaviour and the capacity to plan actions.

With the advance of minimally invasive surgical techniques such as functional stereotactic neurosurgery, physicians were able to destroy with high precision much smaller areas of brain involved in emotional control. These small lesions have virtually no effect on intellectual or emotional spheres, and are generally very effective in controlling violent behaviour.

Since 1970's, development of radio surgery has allowed surgeons to remove tiny bits of brain tissue without opening the skull. Surgeons are now able to pinpoint with great accuracy areas, nuclei, or fibres inside the brain by high-tech methods. However, the indications for such surgery are highly selective and only 200 surgeries are performed every year in USA.[1]

It is obvious from this historical review and latest update of psycho-surgery that its scope is extremely limited. It is indicated

---

1. *The History of Psychosurgery* by Renato M.E. Sabbatini, Ph.D.; http: www.epub.org.br/cm/n02/historia psicocirg_i.htm)

only in mental abnormalities which cannot be cured or controlled by anti-psychotic drugs or psychotherapy. Needless to state that such procedures cannot have anything to do with spiritual experience, life, or phenomenon.

Religion is not merely spiritual experience. It means complete transformation of personality—even changing the whole physiology. Conquest of lust, greed and anger are essential parameters of spiritual evolution. Can this be attained artificially through surgery? Although greed, lust, anger and similar other emotions are considered evil and hindrances to spiritual life, the solution does not consist in destroying them altogether. They must be transmuted and sublimated. Destroying the neural centres responsible for these will be like killing a restive, uncontrolled horse rather than breaking it. These emotions are forces which must be sublimated. Anger must be carefully controlled and directed against those factors which stand as hindrance in spiritual life. Lust means desire for union, and it must be directed towards God.

Psycho Bio-chemistry

Bio-chemistry is another branch with the help of which neuro-scientists have tried to understand the psychic phenomenon. Scientists have identified certain chemicals called neuro-transmitters and neuro-modulators. These substances are released at the nerve junctions and act by altering the electric potentials of the cell membrane. They not only transmit the message, they also selectively facilitate some and inhibit some other information

Different types of neuro-receptors are present in different parts of the brain and this can account for complex and multiple effects of medication, meditation, concentration and contemplation. For example, a subtype of "glutamate receptor" appears to mediate the function of brain plasticity, a process considered important in learning and memory.

Acetyl Choline helps in memory, motivation, perception and cognition. Another neuro-modulator is serotonine. Its increase can produce hallucinations, as happens after LSD intake. Variations in serotonine content affect behaviour, arousal and sleep pattern. Another neuro-transmitter, nor-epinephrine, causes changes in mood—excess leading to elation, and deficiency causing depression. Excess of dopamine levels lead to schizophrenia and psychosis.

Most of the anti-psychotic drugs act through one or more of the above chemicals. The question however, is, "Can any of the available drugs help in the spiritual life or produce a genuine spiritual experience?"

The drugs acting on the mind are of various types. The hard drugs like morphine and heroine produce severe psychological dependence, and are banned. Tobacco, alcohol and certain sedatives are less dependence producing and are used incidentally. Then there are the tranquillizers which have a calming and soothing effect. Of these, major ones are used in psychoses, while minor anxiolytics and anti-depressants are the most commonly prescribed by the physicians in medical practise.

There is a group of drugs called psychodysleptics, which produce hallucinations, alter the sense of time, make sensations more vivid, and obstruct memory revival.

LSD and marijuana are often called "mind manifesting". The experience produced by them is often weird and unpredictable. It leads to lethargy and social passivity. Some of these drugs are unfortunately used non-medically for relief of anxiety and tension, and at times for "fun", amusement, and what is called "kick".

It is a custom among some of the traditional religious sects to use some of these drugs for spiritual purposes. It is true that these drugs may give a spiritual experience like feeling. But as has already been stated, spirituality is not merely an isolated experience or feeling. It is an extremely complex phenomenon which includes transformation of character itself. These drugs can't produce that. On the contrary, prolonged, habitual use of these drugs may lead not only to dependence, but also to moral debasement and depressed sensitivity. Let it be understood clearly: There is not shortcut to spiritual life.

Genetic Engineering and Spiritual Phenomenon

In 1989 the USA launched a spectacular multi-billion research project called 'Human Genome Project' to reveal the entire human genetic code. Its aim is "human enhancement" by planned alteration of genetic codes. Genetic engineering and alteration in genetic codes has already been used to produce hybrid plants and cereals. It is also known that there are certain genetic diseases where a defective or abnormal gene in the patients' chromosomes is responsible for the disease. It has been envisaged, therefore, to achieve cure of diseases by modifying the genetic code.

So far so good. But more ambitiously, the bio-technological scientists plan to produce hybrid humans through genetic engineering! This very idea poses a number of important questions: Is such tampering ethical? Can human advancement be achieved purely by tempering at the physical level? Can matter be the cause of mind? Can human evolution be hastened by genetic engineering? Can a Buddha or a Gandhi, or worse, a Hitler be produced in laboratory? And if this were at all possible, what will happen if such a bio-technique falls in the hands of some unscrupulous person with scant concern for social welfare? Cloning and test tube babies are other areas in which bio-technology is trying to interfere with the natural phenomenon of birth.

It is interesting to note that Indian mythology presents a number of instances of bio-technological interferences, especially in the process of birth. We have, for example, the case of life produced from dead matter: Ganesh was born out of the bodily dust of Mother Parvati. Bhagavatam describes that there was a tyrant king Vena who had to be killed. But he had no heir. So the Brahmins churned his dead body, out of which a dark dwarf with evil propensities arose. Then came out a divine couple. The male became king Prithu and ruled for long.

The second phenomenon is birth of Draupadi and Dristadyumna through yajna —a case of birth without parents. Sri Rama and his three brothers were born when the milk obtained from yajna was fed to the mothers. Here, although mothers are there, there is no contribution of the father, and no sexual union. Mother Mary too conceived immaculately to give birth to Jesus.

Then there is the interesting case of transference of embryo from the womb of one mother to that of the other. According to Jain mythology, the soul of the prophet Mahavir first got embodied as an embryo in the womb of a Brahmin mother. However, the gods transferred it into the womb of a Kshatriya mother, a queen. A similar transference of the embryo of Balaram from the womb of Devaki to that of Rohini is described in the Bhagavatam.

Cases of growth and nurturing of a fertilized ovum outside the mother's womb-equivalent to test-tube babies is also found in Indian mythology. The embryo of the Kauravas emerged from the womb of Gandhari in the form of a single egg. It was kept in an incubator outside the womb. But when it did not grow into a baby for a long time, in desperation it was broken into hundred pieces each one of which became one Kaurava prince. The embryo of sage Agasthya too hatched outside the womb, in a pitcher.

Then, there are stories of duplication of bodies—similar bodies having being produced from one body, akin to cloning. Sage Kardama produced with the help of yogic power nine bodies identical to his own. Raktabija was the demon out of each drop of whose blood one similar demon was born. Finally, there are a number of examples of resorting to yajna, tapas (austerities) or yoga for obtaining progeny of one's own choice.

Thus in Indian religious tradition the possibility of unnatural occurrences and interference in the natural biological processes has not been denied. But they have never been encouraged or given undue importance. Such interferences are unpredictable in their results and may even prove dangerous. Instead, it is always much safer to resort to yogic practices, yajna or tapas to modify the normal or natural biological processes.

So far genetic engineering has only been able to alter the physical characteristics of the living organism. It is yet to be seen whether it can affect the mental characteristics. For this, to begin with, the bio-scientists will have to identify the genes responsible for mental traits like lust, greed, love, compassion, hatred, etc. They may well study the genetic structure of sages and seers, and compare them with those of sinners and criminals. And then would arise the question of the applicability of such a knowledge. Even theoretically it is difficult to accept the principle that matter can produce mind, and it is still more improbable that change in the physical structure would change mind in a predictable manner. In all probability, genetic engineering would also end up with giving us a few more methods for treating some mental diseases. It is always far safer and wiser to resort to yogic, psychological and spiritual techniques for mental transformation.

Evolution and Bio-technology

If we were to accept Darwin's Theory of Evolution, man has evolved out of a mollusc or an amoeba. Darwin certainly does not say anything about the evolution of life out of matter. He only traces the evolution of life-forms. As a matter of fact, although Einstein has been able to give us an equation to describe the relation between matter and energy ($E = mc^2$), no scientist has so far been able to discover an equation between mind and matter, and unless this is defined, every attempt at tempering with matter to influence mind would remain unpredictable.

The next great leap in evolution was when the nerve tissue was evolved. Initially it was merely like a nerve net in Hydra, but later evolved into two nerve cords, leading to a single nerve cord. This again got differentiated in the front to form a nerve ganglion. This again divided into three parts: the fore brain, the mid brain and the hind brain. As evolution proceeded, the fore brain evolved into neo-cerebrum, being the seat of intellect; mid brain became limbic system and thalamus, the seats of emotion and instinct respectively; and the hind brain formed the medulla, the seat for centres for vital functions like respiration and heart beats. In humans, the fore brain or the neo-cerebrum is far more developed than in animals, signifying that in humans intellect plays a far more dominant role than in lower animals.

Now the vital question is: what is the next step in human evolution? Some have envisaged a superman. What is the biological speciality of such a superman? Will he have a special structure or part added to his already evolved brain? Or, will there be only a functional change and not anatomical, in his brain? But before we venture even to give some speculative answers to these questions, we must at least define a "superman," in philosophical, psychological, sociological and spiritual terms. Modern material sciences have no clear idea of a superman. However, all religious traditions of the world have not only clearly defined a "superman", they all owe their very origin to such a divine being. Buddha and Christ, Zoroaster and Ramakrishna, and the like are the prototype of the next stage of human evolution. All the scriptures of the world clearly delineate the characteristics of such a super or divine being. And the human evolution is progressing towards it.

In terms of psychology, some prefer to use "yogic consciousness" as the next step in evolution. Although the very concept of consciousness is vague, modern psychologists have tried to understand it with the help of biology. They associate the concept of consciousness with the evolving nerve tissue in the species. Mukhopadhyaya credits consciousness only to the brain and not to the neural tissue below the brain level. According to him there is a brain-stem consciousness related to waking and sleep states; the mid brain or limbic system consciousness concerned with our instincts and emotions, and finally the cortical consciousness associated with our intellect. He postulates that the higher consciousness in the process of evolution is supra-cortical consciousness.[1]

Psychologists also claim that the two hemispheres of the brain have different psycho and physiological functions. To this, they have given the name bi-modal consciousness. The non-dominant hemisphere is supposed to have functions which are more holistic. However, they are not able to say as yet what the anatomical locus of yogic consciousness is. And unless these issues are answered and clarified, the role of bio-technology cannot possibly be assessed. Some speculations as to the alteration in the structure and function of brain which might be associated with the evolution of a yogic consciousness are postulated by Dr.C.S.Shah:

---

1. Dr. A.K. Mukhopadhyaya, Paper presented at the NCERT seminar 1987, quoted by Shah, C.S.

(a) Certain centres in the brain may be suppressed, while others may get stimulated.

(b) Dormant connections between the nerve cells may be opened.

(c) New connections might develop between the brain cells and the centres.

(d) Quality and quantity of neuro-transmitting chemicals which transfer messages from one cell to another may be altered

(e) New centres may develop, as has happened in human beings during the evolutionary leap from ape to man.

Dr.Shah further suggests, quoting reliable authorities, that brain has great plasticity and its structure can be altered by training, upbringing and experience. We must look for this, rather than something embedded in genes. While natural evolution takes thousands of years to effect such changes, some people can achieve the same results in a few years through conscious and deliberate meditative efforts to control the mind.[1]

---

1. See Shah, Dr.C.S., *Physiology of a Man of God, Part III,* The Vedanta Kesari, August 1999. p311-313.

Conclusion

It cannot be denied that the investigations of modern bio-sciences into the realm of religion and spirituality have helped in understanding the spiritual phenomenon, and to dispel the clouds of mystery around mystic happenings. We have also understood the limitations of bio-technology in bringing about spiritual experiences or in helping in hastening the process of spiritual evolution. It is also a fact that spiritual phenomenon is essential not only for individual fulfillment, it also plays a major role in social well-being. Such scientific inquiries further strengthen the view that spiritual life must be led in right earnestness if we seek personal emancipation, welfare of the society and ascent of the human race to the higher ladder of evolution. Yoga and not bio-technology is the path to higher consciousness. Robots may have their utility, but they are not substitutes for rishis. What we need today are rishis in scores, hundreds and thousands.

Ethical Considerations in Health[1]

(The Sion Foundation asked few questions to each participant at the beginning of the symposium. The answers were sent to all the participants and they were asked to respond to them in the second written symposium)

Answers to the open questions

Q.1. To what extent is one allowed to go in instigating (medical) intervention in the process of birth, life and death? This relates to intervention in one's own life and in that of others.

A: By medical intervention is meant:

(a) to prevent, delay or hasten birth; modify the quality of the offspring artificially by medical means at the individual or the collective level; (b) to alter the quality and

---

1. Contribution of the author to the first written symposium in the Sion Conference on "Ethical Considerations in Health", organized by the Sion Foundation, Netherlands, in 1990-1991.

duration of life during health and illness with the help of drugs; (c) to hasten or delay death, or to make it less painful by medical means.

Intervention in life

Man has been intervening in the process of life and death in all cultures. This interference may be medical or non-medical. Medical intervention takes place in the form of an attempt to improve the quality of life and to prolong its duration.

According to Indian culture, bliss and immortality are the two highest aspirations of man, and disease, old age and death are the greatest hindrances in man's search for everlasting bliss. Hence one must be allowed to instigate medical intervention to achieve the twin objectives of alleviation of suffering and avoidance of death. Any attempt which fails to fulfill these two objectives or threatens to the contrary must be avoided.

Medical intervention is sought for immediate alleviation of suffering as well as for long term gains. Those procedures which yield more lasting results must be preferred.

Again, health and happiness of the community must be emphasized over that of the individual. Unfortunately in the present unjust world facilities and possibilities for medical interventions for prolonging and improving the quality of life are not equally available to all. According to a recent World Bank report, inspite of an optimistic estimate of economic growth, there will be 600 million people in the developing countries trapped in absolute poverty in the year 2000 AD. This is defined as a condition of life so characterized by malnutrition, illiteracy, disease, high infant mortality and low life expectancy as to be beneath any reasonable definition of human decency. Under these appalling situations can few privileged individuals (or nations) be allowed to enjoy excessive use of medical facilities for modifying their life-process to make it more pleasurable when a fraction of the amount of money so spent can prevent thousands of infants from death due to malnutrition and dehydration?

It is equally important to remember the limitations of medical intervention. Since no everlasting happiness is possible at the physical level, medical intervention can produce only impermanent results. A heroic cardiac transplant operation can at the most prolong the life of an individual by a few years, but it cannot guarantee happiness. Peace and happiness depend upon the state of the mind. One can learn to be happy without seeking medical support. Nor can medical means help man to achieve immortality. But man can attain to eternal life by religion and spirituality. Indian culture lays emphasis not on longevity but upon the quality of life. A short life spent in the service of God and one's fellow beings is considered far superior to a long life spent only in selfish pursuits of happiness.

Since the second part of the question seeks to relate it to oneself, I ask myself: If I were to get a coronary artery disease necessitating a sophisticated coronary by-pass operation costing about $5000, what will I do? My answer is that I would forgo the operation and spend the amount in providing a nutritious diet, say two ounces of milk per day to the poorest children in the slums of a developing country.

Intervention in birth

The question of medical intervention in the process of birth is more difficult to answer. Birth can be avoided by preventing conception. But once conception has occurred, medical intervention must be invited only to obtain and ensure the safe birth of a healthy child. In developing countries, specially India, population control by birth-control and family planning has become an ethical necessity to ensure a better quality of life.

Termination of pregnancy by medically induced abortion and thus prevention of birth of a viable child poses a number of socio-ethical problems. It is not generally encouraged in orthodox cultures and communities and is considered sinful. It can be resorted to on strictly medical grounds, for example, if the birth of the child threatens the life of the mother etc. Only recently abortion has been legalized in India.

There is an interesting reference in Jain mythology of the transference of the embryo from the womb of one mother to that of another. According to the legend, the embryo of Lord Mahavir, the 24th prophet of the Jains, was transferred from the womb of a Brahmin mother to that of a queen by the god Indra. This is the solitary example of such an act and had occurred in the special case of a prophet.

Its significance in the present context when artificial implantation of the fertilized ovum has become possible is difficult to assess.

Interference in death

Medical intervention in death is done often quite unnecessarily. Ethical questions arise in making use of medical means in prolonging a painful and useless life. In such cases the socio-psychological importance of the suffering person and his desire to survive must be taken into consideration. Sometimes the very presence of an aged, dependant and invalid grandparent may be the source of great strength and stability to the whole family. Such a life is worth prolonging. A venerable sage lying paralysed and unable to speak even, may still be a source of spiritual benediction for hundreds of devotees.

At the other extreme are the cases of unnecessary spending of large amount of money on terminal care when no reasonable expectation of useful life is possible. One study showed that no less than $35 billion or about 17% of all health expenditure in USA was spent on the care of the terminally ill. There can hardly be a more terrible reflection on the futility and indulgence of modern medicine than this; and of our roles as physicians to struggle so pointlessly, so cleverly, and so expensively to keep people alive; and of our roles as patients to refuse to accept that ultimately we too must die. In our determination to grasp even a few more days or even hours of life, we use resources that are badly needed elsewhere in the community and the world.

Indian culture teaches not only an ideal way of life but also the ideal manner of death. In fact a devout person in India prepares throughout life for an ideal, peaceful death as described in the scriptures.

Traditionally monastic communities in India do not encourage medical intervention in the process of life and death. During illness minimal intervention is sought and a monk prefers to forbear pain and suffering as part of penance and surrender to the will of God. Illness and suffering are seen as expiations of past evil karma and therefore considered welcome. So also is death accepted as a welcome deliverer of the soul from its imprisonment in the human body. Many monks are known to patiently forbear intense and prolonged pain of diseases like cancer without taking analgesics and without wishing for an early death. This religious approach of a monk towards life and death has influenced the society at large also and many non-monastic lay people also adopt a similar attitude towards them.

Voluntary termination of life by fasting or by other scripturally prescribed means is allowed for Hindu and Jain monks under certain conditions. Every devout Jain aspires to attain "Samadhi-marana", or death while in meditation by gradual fasting. Under normal conditions it is undertaken if there is terminal or incurable illness or in old age when body has lost all its usefulness. The author, being the product of Indian culture, aspires for the glorious death in meditation.

For all those who are not ready to face death so heroically as mentioned above, medical intervention may be sought to ensure as painless a death as possible.

The question of euthanasia is far more complicated and debatable and has many ethical and legal problems attached to it.

Q.2. Most essential ethical question in the realm of health and illness.

A. The ethical problems confronting a doctor who plays the key role in the sphere of health and illness vary according to place, person and situation. However, there are certain common global problems posed by present technological advancements in the medical fields which doctors in all countries are facing.

Medicine, both diagnostic and therapeutic, has become extremely expensive. In USA illness and disease cause great financial stress on the non-affluent persons and are the major causes of bankruptsy. The influx of modern western medical norms and knowledge, together with expensive modern technological diagnostic apparatus and therapeutic procedures into the developing countries have posed similar problems there too. In this context the most important ethical question which I would like to discuss with my colleagues and participants from other nations is: "To what extent must economic considerations be allowed to influence decision-making regarding diagnostic procedure and treatment?"

This question can be stated differently as follows: "Can medical profession be freed from monetary constraints?" or "How can the cost of diagnosis and treatment of the sick be reduced to the minimum?"

Q.3. Let me elaborate the question and its possible answer in the form of a hypothetical case history:

A high school teacher, belonging to the lower middle economic class in India comes to me for pain in abdomen, weakness and loss of appetite of three months' duration. On enquiring the personal and family history I am told that he has two daughters and a son and earns Rs.1000 (approx. $75) per month. He has to look after his family as well as two aged parents with this meagre income.

On examination I find that the patient's liver is enlarged. A number of diagnostic possibilities come to my mind. To arrive at an exact diagnosis I must carry out a number of investigations including biochemical examination of blood, special x-ray and ultrasonographic tests etc. which may cost approximately Rs.1000. That would mean a serious strain on the meagre financial reserves of the patient. Now the question before me is:

Should I order these investigations or should I treat the patient empirically on the basis of the clinical data alone? As a scientist I must get the necessary investigations done.

At the same time as a humanitarian I must keep the financial load to the minimum. A number of alternative ways are before me:

(i) Refer the patient to a charitable hospital/laboratory where facilities for the required investigations are available, free of cost or at minimum charges.

(ii) Request some laboratory to do the investigations on charity basis.

(iii) Bear the expenses of investigations and treatment personally or collectively by forming a charitable trust.

(iv) Initiate political action with a view to prevent medical science from becoming a business or pure science bereft of all humanitarian considerations.

The hypothetical case sited above represents the typical situation which I have to face every day in my practice. I try to solve the problem in one of the first three ways mentioned above. I would like to know the reaction of the other participants and their solutions to the problem.

Contribution to the Second and Final written Symposium

The contribution of the various learned participants are diverse and cover a large spectrum of ideas reflecting the differences in cultures and ethical problems. It is gratifying to note that many participants have raised wider and basic issues, like tendency to over-medication, mechanistic approach towards health and disease, economic considerations influencing ethical decisions, need to emphasize preventive medicine, compassion towards animals, etc. One participant has equated morality with politics. Arguing in this strain, ethics does not remain a simple code of personal conduct but becomes more generalized and universal. Beginning with isolated problems of medical ethics as applicable to individual cases, a physician gets involved into socio-economics of patients and may even enter into politics and influence policy-making in matters of health. It depends upon the individual physician at what level he should act in solving the ethical problems.

In the present age the world has become a united whole which can no longer be divided into isolated regions. No individual can remain or keep himself isolated, insulated from the global events and thought processes. Hence what we can do is to evolve some general principles of ethics in the framework of which wide variety of modifications can be allowed according to individual cases, cultural settings and specific situations. A healthy ethical system must have general rules as well as particular exceptions. It must have absolute, ideal, inviolable ethical principles as well as relative, practical, flexible moral rules. Both balance and complement each other. They both serve the common goal of material and spiritual welfare of the individual and the society.

'Sanctity of Life' could be one such general or universal ethical principle. Life must include not only all viable human life but even human sperm-life, foetal life, and the life of animals, insects and the plant kingdom. Just as an unborn foetus has a right to survive, animals and plants too have every right to survive. It is important to develop a sense of respect for everything living. None must unnecessarily or without valid reason destroy any life, be it as insignificant as a blade of grass. Violence in all forms must be eschewed from our thought and action.

Another general guiding principle for all ethical considerations is: "Sacrifice one's self for the family; sacrifice one's family for the sake of the town; sacrifice the town for the nation; nation for the world and the world for the Supreme Spirit which resides in the heart of all creatures."

The western participants have emphasized the dignity of the individual and his right to take decision for himself. Indian culture however lays greater stress on the role of society in decision making in health care. A patient consults all his responsible family members and the leaders and elders of the community before making crucial decisions regarding health. Thus decision making becomes a social affair rather than remaining a purely personal matter in India.

Interference in the process of birth in the form of prevention of conception, abortion or genetic engineering is not encouraged in Indian tradition. Sex as a source of pleasure apart from conception too is not appreciated. Sex is legitimately allowed only for the birth of child, or where such a possibility is accepted. Sex for pleasure alone is considered far too inferior and unworthy attitude. Abstinence from sex as the best means of birth control is highly extolled in Indian tradition. But as long as the majority of humanity does not rise to such high concepts and ideals of self control and learn to derive pleasure in higher pursuits, artificial means of contraception and even abortion may have to be allowed to control the population. In this connection it may be mentioned that the only fool-proof method of prevention of AIDS (which has been advocated by experts in India officially) is abstinence from sex—something which the Indian culture very easily accepts.

Abortion to destroy the embryo or foetus of an unwanted or potentially handicapped child too is not encouraged. A child not wanted by the parents or a physically handicapped or deformed child may yet be a genius. A paraplegic child may grow into a mathematical wizard or may have prodigious memory. Indian tradition abounds in stories and myths highlighting the fact of deformed or unwanted children proving spiritual blessing to the society.

Genetic engineering may not be a safe or fool-proof method of obtaining children of desired quality. A couple may choose a handsome child with fair complexion but it may be mentally dull. A mistake in such engineering procedure may produce a criminal instead of a planned saint, which may prove a curse rather than a blessing to the society. Indian culture suggests other methods of getting the desired type of children. A whole science involving incantations, special rituals and meditations is developed in India to obtain children of special quality. A mother desiring a god-fearing child listens to stories of saints and sages, and spends her days of pregnancy in performing devotional exercises. Another mother seeking a warrior child engages in listening and reading stories of wars and warriors and so on.

Personal questions put forward by the SION office

1. In your first contribution you outline the problems involved with the fair distribution of medical facilities. You state that there are few possibilities for cheap medical help in your country, a problem which plays a role in all decisions taken in your medical practice. You also present a good picture as to the place and significance of medical intervention in Indian culture.

For a better understanding of your way of thinking, would you indicate how the fair distribution of medical facilities is realized (and was realized in the past) in the Indian culture and what the views according to Indian tradition are in this respect.

2. Can you explain what, according to Indian (medical) tradition, the feelings are towards deciding on priorities (which patient should be treated first, etc.)?

3. You refer to the mythological legend of Mahavir in your contribution. We feel that such a legend could be a valuable contribution to the SION conference. Could you elucidate this legend in more detail? Are there any other myths in your culture which relate to the ethical problems discussed in your contribution?

Answers to your questions

Q.1. How fair distribution of medical facilities is realized (and was realized in the past) in the Indian culture and what the views according to Indian tradition are in this respect?

1. As has already been pointed out in my first communication, mental and spiritual health had always been stressed in Indian culture. Accordingly there had never been such over-emphasis on, and

preoccupation with physical health as it is in the west today. People generally disregarded minor symptoms and allowed nature to take its own course in the initial phases of the illness. They did not approach doctor for minor ailments. This may have some disadvantages but it does prevent unnecessary investigations and over-medication.

2. A large number of effective household remedies were known to all, even to the housewives, who successfully used them to treat minor ailments of the members of the family, especially children. Common medicinal herbs and plants were grown in the private garden of the house.

3. The priest, the teacher and the physician never demanded fee for their services. To charge fee for such services was considered sacrilegious. Medical profession was considered very noble and, like learning, medical help too was imparted free of cost. It was the duty of the State to provide for the livelihood of the physician. In lieu of his services, the priest, the teacher and the physician received what was called *dakshina*—a voluntary gift made by the

beneficiary at the completion of the course of treatment, or study, etc. This gift naturally depended upon and varied with the financial status of the treated person. Such physicians who never 'sold' their skill nor used it to earn money were highly respected in the society and never suffered from any want. The commitment of the State to protect and provide the needs of the physician, and the custom of *dakshina* allowed the cost of treatment to remain within the means of all strata in the society. Patients too poor to purchase medicines or give even *dakshina* to the physician were treated free, and at times the physician himself provided medicines also.

4. The problems of unfair distribution of medical facilities has become serious and acute in recent years due to technological advancements, commercialization of medical profession, erosion of ancient ethical values and over-emphasis on physical health. In India, we are struggling in various ways to deal with the problems:

(a) Greater stress has been laid in the government's health policy on preventive medicine.

(b) A scheme has been started for the training of village health workers who would administer preliminary treatment at the village level for minor ailments and refer serious cases to the specialist or the hospital.

(c) Indigenous and household remedies which can be useful for prevention and treatment of minor ailments are being popularized by the government. A number of voluntary agencies are also doing similar work.

(d) Attempts are being made to improvise, alter and modify modern methods of diagnosis and treatment to suit Indian needs and finances.

Q.2. Feeling towards deciding on priorities in medical care:

In a family, the top priority for treatment is given to small children. The next in priority are the elderly, e.g., the grand parents. Every adult in a family thinks of the welfare of others first, and since small children have not developed this sense of duty, they get the first attention. The house-lady traditionally takes her meals after everyone else in the family has been fed.

This attitude is reflected in medical care also. The housewife comes last in the list of priority. This is a natural and voluntary distribution of priority and should not be interpreted as neglect of women.

No society is perfect, and inspite of highest ideals, disparities are often found in practice. There are a number of voluntary bodies which take care of those groups of people who are neglected by the society. The Ramakrishna Mission Home of Service, Varanasi, has a 100 years old tradition of giving top priority in providing medical help to the most neglected and the poorest among the city-dwellers. Persons lying uncared for on the road-side due to poverty, neglect, old age or sickness used to be picked up by the monks of this institution and were treated with highest care and dedication. Unfortunately this noble feeling in deciding on priority is being altered by the rapid sociological changes.

Among diseases, those which are serious, which are likely to have a protracted course and which produce many complications are given priority in being treated. According to ancient Indian medical law, a physician must not undertake the treatment of incurable or terminal diseases.

Q.3. Myths and legends related to birth, embryo transfer, etc.:

Legend of the birth of Lord Mahavir, the Jain prophet

According to Jain tradition, an arhat or prophet is never born in lowly, destitute, or miserly clans or in the caste of brahmanas. But it is possible that a prodigious exception might occur and an arhat or prophet might enter for a short time the womb of a woman from an undeserving clan owing to the potency of an enduring, yet-to-be-destroyed karma. Due to a very small particle of impure karma yet to be destroyed, the soul of Lord Mahavir entered the womb of the brahmana lady named Devananda.

When Indra, the king of gods, learnt about it, he decided in accordance with the established practice, to transfer the embryo of the arhat or prophet to the womb of a woman belonging to a noble bred clan. Indra therefore ordered one of his subordinate gods, Harinaigameshi, to carry the embryo of Mahavir from the womb of Devananda to that of Trishala, a kshatriya lady, and likewise transfer the embryo in the womb of Trishala to the womb of Devananda.

The process by which Harinaigameshi performed the transfer of the two embryos is described in details in Kalpa Sutra, the Jain scripture. First, he underwent two transformations himself. He removed the gross and evil elements from his own body and assumed a pure body other than his original one. Thereafter, travelling with lightening speed, he reached the place where Devananda was residing. He first saluted the embryo of Lord Mahavir. He then hypnotized Devananda and her attendants into deep sleep. After this he removed the evil and unholy particles present there, and showered around the particles of holiness. After seeking permission of Lord Mahavir, he gently lifted the embryo on his palms and carried it to where Trishala lived. He first hypnotized Trishala and her attendants into sleep and purified the place and Trishala's body by removing evil and showering holy particles. He then gently placed Lord Mahavir's embryo in the womb of Trishala, and removed the embryo which was in her womb, to be transferred to Devananda's womb.

Lord Mahavir was aware that he will be transferred, was not aware of the transfer, but was aware later that he had been transferred. The transfer took place at midnight, and eighty two days after he had entered the womb of Devananda.

This legend has elements which reconcile the doctrine of karma and the theory of hereditary transmission. The detailed procedure involved in embryo transfer finds some parallels with modern surgical operation.

The Story of Ashtavakra

A sage was chanting holy texts in the presence of his pregnant wife. The foetus in the womb of the lady, on hearing the chant spoke from inside the womb that the intonations were not correct. This enraged the sage. He cursed his son in the womb that since he had a crooked mind, let his body too become crooked. The story says that the child was born with eight deformities (Ashtavakra) in his body, but was intellectually brilliant.

The Story of Abhimanyu

Arjuna, the great hero of the Mahabharata war had a prodigious son, Abhimanyu, who had learnt a special military secret while in the womb, when his father had described it to his mother. But since the mother fell asleep and did not listen to the whole secret, Abhimanyu too obtained partial knowledge. With the help of this knowledge, he was able to break the special army formation of the enemy called 'chakravyuha', and enter into it. But due to incomplete knowledge, he could not come out of it, and was killed.

The Story of Ashwatthama

Ashwatthama out of intense hatred for the righteous Pandavas fired the deadly and infallible weapon called 'Brahmastra', to destroy the embryo of Parikshita, the lone successor of the Pandavas. The embryo was saved by Sri Krishna, the incarnate Lord. For his unpardonable act of trying to destroy the embryo, which is considered the greatest sin, Ashwatthama was cursed with extreme suffering for an infinite period of time with an open, painful wound on the forehead.

Brahma is mythologically considered the god of intellect. *Brahmastra* therefore means the weapon or instrument obtained as a gift of intellect. The legend of Ashwatthama is thus symbolic of the use of intelligence for the destruction of the embryo/foetus, which is considered as an unpardonable sin.

The above legends show that although it is possible to modify the foetus in the womb, it is not free from danger. Such actions may change the very course of history.

There are other legends which describe the process of incubation of the embryo or parts of it outside the mother's womb under special circumstances. There are also legends in which the head of an animal like elephant or goat is transplanted on the trunk of a person whose head had been severed.